GEORGIA'S HISTORIC RESTAURANTS

and their recipes

JOHN F. BLAIR, *Publisher*
Winston-Salem, North Carolina

GEORGIA'S HISTORIC RESTAURANTS

and their recipes

by **DAWN O'BRIEN**
and **JEAN SPAUGH**

Drawings by Debra L. Hampton

Copyright© 1987 by Dawn O'Brien and Jean Spaugh
Printed in the United States of America
All rights reserved
Book design by Virginia Ingram
Drawings by Debra L. Hampton
Cover Photographs by Bernard Carpenter
Composition by Superior Typesetters, Inc.
Manufactured by Donnelley Printing Company

Library of Congress Cataloging-in-Publication Data

O'Brien, Dawn.
Georgia's historic restaurants and their recipes.

Includes index.
1. Cookery, American—Southern style. 2. Cookery—Georgia. 3. Restaurants, lunch rooms, etc.—Georgia—Guide-books. 4. Historic buildings—Georgia.
I. Spaugh, Jean.   II. Title.
TX715.0283 1987   641.509758   87-20951
ISBN 0-89587-056-8

DEDICATION

I would like to dedicate my part of this book to my best friend, Betty Jo Gilley. B.J., like a firefly, lit up the darkness with her magic.

    Dawn O'Brien

I'd like to thank sweet Richard Spaugh, whom I am nominating for sainthood.

    Jean Christopher Spaugh

ACKNOWLEDGMENTS

Georgia is a beautiful state that overflows with caring people. They care about their heritage and work to see that it is preserved. And, in our case, we found that a surprising number of people were willing to share their knowledge and experiences with us. We received help not only from the expected places, but also from many unexpected sources. We are grateful for the help of so many people, but would particularly like to thank the following:

To: The restaurateurs and chefs who gave us good stories, good food and good recipes.

To: Deva Hirsch at the Tourist Division of the Georgia Department of Industry and Trade and to tourism representatives Becky Aliff, Becky Bassett, Jeannie Buttrum, Mary Jo Murrah, Kitty Peoples, Gail Smith, Carol Spires and Dawn Townsend.

To: Jenny Stacy of the Savannah Convention and Visitors Bureau.

To: Sheryl Johnson of the Georgia Visitors Center.

To: The artist, Debbie Hampton, for translating photos into works of art.

To: Ronnie Thomas, who crisscrossed Georgia with me, faithfully scanning the map and saying, "I think we should have turned back there."

To: Jeannette Christopher, who taught me history and cooking and still corrects my grammar.

To: Saxton Powell and Betty Jo Gilley for helping with the testing and retesting of recipes.

To: The guinea pig recipe tasters who stroke our and the chefs' egos with their effusive compliments and instructional criticisms.

FOREWORD

All of us have some special interest that sparks a gleam in our eyes, some subject we can wax eloquently on—or at least wish that we had the right words to do it justice. For me, that special thing is historic restaurants that serve good food.

When it became apparent, after researching and writing two books on the subject, that I needed collaborators for the books that would follow, I knew exactly what sort of person I needed. I had to find someone (for each book) who would feel the elation I feel when discovering a historic restaurant. I needed someone who, after biting into a sweet, ripe piece of fruit, would roll the flavor about the tongue, trying to capture the flavor, the particular essence of the fruit *so she or he could describe it to someone else*. In other words, a writer. Fortunately, I have been lucky to find collaborators who not only share my passion concerning history and cuisine but who can write also.

My collaborator for this book was Jean Spaugh. By the time we were midway through our travels in Georgia, Jean was amazed at the incredible variety of historic restaurants and at the heterogenous mix of cuisine we found. Take the terms *continental* or *down-home cooking*. They vary not only from state to state but also from region to region within the same state. Each restaurant has its own brand of cuisine, but more than that, each has its own architecture, history and amusing stories to tell. Those differences are a big part of why it has been so much fun for me to follow *North Carolina's Historic Restaurants and Their Recipes* with books on Virginia, South Carolina, Maryland, Pennsylvania and now Georgia and Florida.

For those of you not familiar with any of the other books, let me explain the criteria Jean and I used in our selection of restaurants. Generally, the building housing the restaurant had to be at least fifty years old, or reconstructed of materials more than fifty years old on a historically significant site. Our criteria are less rigorous and complex than those of the National Register of Historic Buildings, but we follow their basic approach to what defines a historic building.

The other standards we use have to do with the food, atmosphere and service, and we readily admit that these factors are as subjective as they are objective. So, if one of your favorite historic restaurants is not in this book, there could be many reasons for the omission. We had to limit the number to fifty; some restaurants weren't interested in participating; others didn't want to divulge their recipes. And, occasionally, we received recipes that we couldn't get to come out right even after we'd tested them several times. So, we deleted that restaurant. After all, our book is basically for home cooks, and if we can't make a dish taste as it did in the restaurant, we don't want you to waste your time on it either.

Georgia's historic restaurants make good memories. Whenever you are traveling in Georgia, whether across a city or across the state, take every opportunity to visit these delightful places. And when you can't go yourself, just make one of the scrumptious recipes in your own kitchen. If your family is anything like Jean's and mine, they'll love tasting new and unusual dishes. Jean's family now regularly demands the Rankin Quarter's Banana Fluff. And my husband keeps asking when I'm going to make LaPrade's Cabbage Cheese again. I'll bet you'll discover many dishes that will become a tradition in your own home. Bon appétit! Or, as my children would say, "Chow down!"

CONTENTS

Foreword — x

THE STOVALL HOUSE — 1
Sautee

LAPRADE'S — 5
Clarkesville

TAYLOR'S TROLLEY — 9
Clarkesville

THE SOUTHERN TRACE — 13
Lavonia

RUDOLPH'S ON GREEN STREET — 17
Gainesville

THE WOODBRIDGE INN — 21
Jasper

THE TATE HOUSE — 25
Tate

THE OLD MILL RESTAURANT — 29
Cedartown

LICKSKILLET FARM — 33
Alpharetta

THE PUBLIC HOUSE ON ROSWELL SQUARE — 37
Roswell

MAXIMILLIAN'S — 41
Marietta

THE PLANTERS RESTAURANT — 45
Marietta

THE MANSION — 49
Atlanta

ANTHONY'S PLANTATION RESTAURANT — 53
Atlanta

HERREN'S AND GUIDO'S 57
Atlanta

LE PAPILLON RESTAURANT 61
IN INMAN PARK
Atlanta

ATKIN'S PARK RESTAURANT 65
Atlanta

THE ABBEY 69
Atlanta

HARRY BISSETT'S NEW ORLEANS 73
CAFE & OYSTER BAR
Athens

FOX HOLLOW 77
Madison

THE DEPOT AT COVINGTON 81
Covington

THE VERANDA 85
Senoia

SOMETHING SPECIAL 89
Newnan

IN CLOVER 93
LaGrange

OAK TREE RESTAURANT 97
Hamilton

BLUDAU'S GOETCHIUS HOUSE 101
Columbus

THE RANKIN QUARTER 105
Columbus

THE FARMHOUSE 109
Ellerslie

THE VICTORIAN TEA ROOM *Warm Springs*	113
THE HOTEL UPSON *Thomaston*	117
THE LEFT BANQUE *Forsyth*	121
BEALL'S 1860 *Macon*	125
NEW PERRY HOTEL AND MOTEL *Perry*	129
SUSINA PLANTATION INN *Thomasville*	133
THE NEEL HOUSE *Thomasville*	137
NAN'S *Valdosta*	141
THE ATTIC *Waycross*	145
BLUEBERRY HILL *Hoboken*	149
SEAGLE'S *St. Mary's*	153
THE KING AND PRINCE BEACH HOTEL AND VILLAS *St. Simon's Island*	157
THE CLOISTER *Sea Island*	161
ELIZABETH ON 37TH *Savannah*	165
THE OLDE PINK HOUSE *Savannah*	169

MRS. WILKES' BOARDING HOUSE   173
Savannah

THE PIRATES' HOUSE   177
Savannah

CHARLES' RESTAURANT   181
Lyons

YE OLDE COFFEE SHOP   185
Louisville

GOLDSMITH'S PULLMAN HALL   189
Augusta

THE KNOX TERRACE DINING ROOM   193
Thomson

ANOTHER THYME   197
Washington

Index   201

THE STOVALL HOUSE
Sautee

THE STOVALL HOUSE

People were on the veranda attentively listening to a storyteller as I approached the old, white clapboard house on a clear summer day. As I stopped for a while to enjoy the story, the rich aroma of lunch drifted out the open windows.

Inside the stunningly renovated home, the highly polished floors and Schwartz family antiques make you feel at home. Seated for lunch on an enclosed porch with a good view of Lynch Mountain, I noticed a child's swing hanging from a massive tree. I thought once again of the storyteller's tale of this house and grounds. The land was once owned by the Cherokees, who were driven off by the white settlers. The settlers drew lots for the land, and Moses Harshaw, reputed to have been the meanest man who ever lived, drew this lot. He built his home here in 1837. In addition to throwing his slaves off Lynch Mountain after they were no longer of use to him, the story goes that he also demanded that his young daughter, who had died when he was away, be exhumed so that he could examine the expensive dress his wife had purchased for her burial clothes. Watching a butterfly land on the swing, I decided that the epitaph on Harshaw's tombstone was fitting: "He is dead and gone to hell."

In the late 1800s, the Stovalls bought the house and added the handsome walnut doors and fireplaces. Then, in order to attract a doctor to northern Georgia, the house was offered to Dr. Walter, who became much beloved for opening his home to the public. That tradition continues under the proprietorship of the Schwartz family, who has converted the attic into charming bedrooms with baths. Although the relaxed atmosphere and the pleasant location enhance a visit to the Stovall House, the best part is the creative cuisine.

Their Ham and Cheddar Phyllo, filled with large chunks of ham and broccoli in a Cheddar cheese sauce, was hearty yet light, and especially delicious. Because a man nearby raved so about his Stuffed Chicken with cream cheese and herbs, I couldn't resist sampling that dish, too, and knew immediately that readers would want to know about this scrumptious creation.

Would I neglect dessert in a place like this? No way! And you shouldn't either, especially if they are serving their wonderful Apple Raisin Pie.

The Stovall House is located on Highway 255, 5 miles east of Helen off Highway 17. Lunch is served from 11:30 a.m. until 2:00 p.m. and dinner from 5:30 p.m. until 8:30 p.m., Tuesday through Saturday. Sunday brunch is served from 10:00 a.m. until 2:00 p.m. For reservations call (404) 878-3355.

THE STOVALL HOUSE'S APPLE RAISIN PIE

5 cups fresh apples, peeled and cored
¾ cup brown sugar
2 tablespoons plain flour
½ teaspoon nutmeg
½ teaspoon cinnamon
¾ cup raisins
1 9-inch pie shell, unbaked

Heat oven to 375 degrees. Slice apples and mix with remaining ingredients. Pour mixture into a 9-inch unbaked pie shell.

Topping:
1 cup plain flour
1 stick cold butter
½ cup sugar

With a pastry cutter, cut butter into the flour and sugar until crumbly. Spread evenly over pie and bake for about 50 minutes or until apples are tender. Yields 1 pie.

THE STOVALL HOUSE'S STUFFED CHICKEN

8 ounces cream cheese
1 teaspoon basil
1 teaspoon chives
1 teaspoon dill
1 clove garlic, crushed
8 boneless chicken breasts, halved
½ cup or more vegetable oil
1 cup flour for dredging
2 eggs, beaten
1 cup bread crumbs

Let cream cheese soften to room temperature. In a small bowl, mix cream cheese with herbs and garlic. Flatten chicken breasts and roll each breast around a dollop (about the size of a walnut) of herbed cheese. Cover and chill for at least 1 hour. Put ¼ inch of oil in skillet and heat to medium. Place flour, eggs and bread crumbs in separate bowls. Dredge chicken in flour, then egg, then bread crumbs. Sauté chicken until lightly browned on all sides. Place chicken on a greased baking sheet and bake at 350 degrees for 30 minutes. Serves 8.

THE STOVALL HOUSE'S HAM AND CHEDDAR PHYLLO

2 tablespoons butter
1 cup all-purpose flour
1 cup milk
2 cups Cheddar or Swiss cheese, grated
4 cups ham, cooked

2 cups chopped broccoli
dash of pepper
dash of cayenne pepper
8 sheets phyllo
⅓ to ½ cup melted butter

In a large skillet, melt butter and add flour. Stir into a smooth roux. Slowly add milk, stirring until well incorporated. Add cheese, ham, broccoli and seasonings. Stir until cheese has melted and flavors have combined.

Lay 1 sheet of phyllo on lightly floured surface. Brush with melted butter. Lay second layer over first. Place about ¼ of filling at the center of phyllo. Fold phyllo into thirds (as you would fold a letter) and seal with butter. Repeat procedure until all phyllo sheets and filling are used. Place on greased cookie sheet, brush top of each phyllo with butter and cook in a 350-degree oven for 10 minutes. Slice while hot and serve. Serves 6 to 8.

LAPRADE'S
Clarkesville

LAPRADE'S

Fishermen on Burton Lake and hunters in the Appalachian Mountains know what the tolling of the bell means at LaPrade's. It announces mealtime! On the morning of my visit, the melodious announcement came at 7:45, and it meant that the long handmade dining tables, covered with practical white vinyl, were about to be laden with an eye-opening country breakfast.

The sun was just breaking through the mountain fog as I sat down beside a flock of hungry people in the wood-paneled dining room. We were served in the family-style manner. Huge platters of Country Ham and Sausage were brought to our table first. These were immediately followed with bowls of Red-eye Gravy, Grits, Scrambled Eggs and plates of hot Biscuits. Sorghum syrup, honey and homemade jellies were eagerly passed as our cups were continually filled with steaming hot coffee.

I tried several different combinations, ladling Red-eye Gravy on my Grits and topping my Biscuits with butter and honey. And like my table mates, I rarely let a full plate pass my way without trying a little bit more Country Ham or Sausage. While we devoured our hearty meal, my friendly neighbors chatted with me. I learned that many had come here as children themselves.

The old fish camp, affectionately known as LaPrade's, began around the turn of the century when John LaPrade bought six hundred acres of land near Burton Lake, which was located in what is now the area north of Goat Island. Back in 1916, the lake was built here to harness the Tallulah River as a power supply. At that time LaPrade built a camp to house and feed the lake's engineers and workers, but after the completion of the lake in 1925, the camp was opened to the public as a fishing retreat. Since then, generations of families have come to stay in the little cabins and dine three times a day in the mountain tradition of garden fresh vegetables, fried chicken, cornbread and good old-fashioned desserts.

After breakfast many guests hurried to get out on the well-stocked lake, but there were a few, like me, who chose to sit out on the porch in the old wooden rockers. One guest told a story of catching a striped bass, a fish (he explained) that is able to eat half of its weight each day. Another guest joined in, "That's not so hard to believe, I just got through doing that in the dining room." I knew exactly what he meant.

LaPrade's is located on Route 1, Highway 197 North, 18 miles from Clarkesville. All meals are served every day but Wednesday. Breakfast is served from 8:00 a.m. until 9:00 a.m.; lunch from 12:30 p.m. until 2:00 p.m.; and dinner from 7:00 p.m. until 8:00 p.m. For reservations (necessary) call (404) 947-3312. LaPrade's is open daily from April 1 until December 1, except in April and November when it is only open on weekends.

LAPRADE'S BAKED APPLES

12 medium, tart apples
1½ cups sugar
1 teaspoon cinnamon
1 teaspoon nutmeg
1 teaspoon allspice
1 stick butter

Core and quarter apples and place in a large, greased baking dish. Mix sugar and spices together and sprinkle evenly over apples. Slice butter in ¼-inch wedges and place evenly over apples. Bake in a preheated 375-degree oven for 45 to 60 minutes or until apples are soft. Serves 6.

LAPRADE'S CABBAGE IN CHEESE SAUCE

1 large head of cabbage
1 teaspoon salt
3 tablespoons butter
2 tablespoons sifted all-purpose flour
1 cup milk
2 cups grated American cheese
1 cup buttered bread crumbs

Core and quarter cabbage and place in a saucepan with salted water. Cover and cook for 10 minutes or until tender. Drain water and place cabbage in a greased casserole dish. Melt butter in a skillet and stir in flour until mixture is smooth.

Add milk and cook over medium heat, stirring constantly until sauce is smooth and thickened. Add cheese and stir until melted. Pour sauce over cabbage and cover evenly with bread crumbs. Bake in a preheated 350-degree oven for 20 minutes or until bread crumbs are brown. Serves 6.

LAPRADE'S POTATO PATTIES

6 medium Kennebec potatoes
1 tablespoon salt
½ tablespoon black pepper
3 ounces all-purpose flour
¼ cup evaporated milk
1 egg
½ stick butter
½ medium Vidalia onion, chopped
1 mild or hot pepper, chopped (optional)
oil

Peel and quarter potatoes and place them in a pot with enough salted water to cover. Cook until tender; then drain. Place in a mixing bowl and mash potatoes with pepper, flour, milk, egg, butter and onions. When well mixed, add mild or hot pepper if desired, and shape mixture into patties. Oil a large, iron frying pan and fit patties into pan. Bake in a 350-degree (preheated) oven until patties are a golden brown on each side. Drain on paper towels. Yields 12 patties.

TAYLOR'S TROLLEY
Clarkesville

TAYLOR'S TROLLEY   Back in 1907, when Clarkesville was a mecca for summer tourists, the trolley could be heard clanging along Washington Street in front of Brewer Drug Store. The trolley brought visitors from the railroad station to the village hotels. Now, some eighty years later, James and Kathleen Taylor have renovated the drugstore, retaining its ceiling fans, handsome soda fountain and beautiful apothecary cabinets.

The establishment no longer looks like a drugstore. There is now a stylish Victorian feel to the décor. The authentically restored wooden cabinets are filled with leather-bound books interspersed with antique silver pieces. Along the back wall, Kathleen has arranged her own emerald green depression glass.

When I sat down for dinner it occurred to me that it had been some time since I had ordered anything from a soda fountain, so I didn't pass up the chance to sip an old-fashioned Vanilla Coke. Before my drink arrived, I cautioned myself that it couldn't possibly taste as good as my memories would insist—but was I ever wrong!

Next, I sampled a tasty Blueberry Muffin, hot from the oven, and a light Fruit Salad. For an entrée, I chose their Hawaiian Chicken. One bite told me that this tangy dish belonged on my recipe list. The desserts at Taylor's Trolley have interesting origins. At this restaurant, the desserts are made from favorite recipes of the guests' grandmothers. Thus my dilemma over velvety Chocolate Chip Cheesecake or Carrot Cake made with pineapple and maple syrup. I solved the dilemma by ordering each and asking for both recipes.

Taylor's Trolley is located at 804 North Washington Street in Clarkesville. Lunch is served from 11:00 a.m. until 3:00 p.m. Monday through Saturday. Dinner is served from 6:00 p.m. until 9:00 p.m. Thursday, Friday and Saturday. For reservations (suggested) call (404) 754-5566.

TAYLOR'S TROLLEY'S HAWAIIAN CHICKEN

2 boneless chicken breasts, skinned
⅓ cup Teriyaki sauce
2 tablespoons butter, melted
¼ cup corn syrup
1 tablespoon vinegar
1 teaspoon salt
1 cup chopped pineapple
¼ cup finely chopped onions
¼ cup finely chopped red and green peppers
⅛ cup pineapple juice
⅛ cup water
2 tablespoons cornstarch
2 pineapple slices

Cook chicken for 5 to 15 minutes over a charcoal grill or in a hot, 425-degree oven, basting with Teriyaki sauce mixed with melted butter. Meanwhile, place the remaining ingredients, except cornstarch and pineapple slices, in a saucepan over simmering heat for about 30 minutes. Add cornstarch and stir until thickened. Spoon sauce over cooked chicken and garnish with pineapple slices. Serves 2.

TAYLOR'S TROLLEY'S CHOCOLATE CHIP CHEESECAKE

Graham Cracker Crust:
1½ cups graham cracker crumbs
1 tablespoon sugar
½ teaspoon cinnamon
½ cup melted butter

Mix all ingredients together and pat crust into the greased bottom and sides of an 8- or 9-inch springform pan.

Filling:
4 8-ounce packages cream cheese
1 cup sugar
4 eggs
1 teaspoon vanilla
1 teaspoon almond extract
¾ cup sour cream
1 12-ounce package chocolate chips

Mix cream cheese and sugar together with an electric mixer. Add eggs, one at a time, and beat until thoroughly mixed. Add vanilla and almond flavoring. Fold in sour cream and chocolate chips. Pour into a springform pan that has already been prepared with a recipe of crust. Bake at 350 degrees for 60 to 70 minutes. Yields 1 cheesecake.

TAYLOR'S TROLLEY'S CARROT CAKE

3¾ cups all-purpose flour
¾ cup brown sugar
1 tablespoon baking powder
1 teaspoon baking soda
¾ teaspoon salt
1 stick butter

6 ounces chopped pecans
4 eggs
¾ cup maple syrup
¾ cup orange juice
3 cups carrots, finely shredded
½ cup crushed pineapple

Preheat oven to 350 degrees and grease 3 9-inch cake pans. Into a large bowl, measure flour, brown sugar, baking powder, baking soda and salt. With a pastry blender, cut in the butter until a fine crumb consistency is reached. Stir in nuts. In a small bowl, beat eggs slightly with a fork. Stir in maple syrup and orange juice until well mixed. Stir the liquid mixture into the flour mixture until moist; mix in pineapple and carrots. Spoon batter into pans and bake for 40 to 50 minutes. Cool in pans for 10 minutes before frosting the cake. Yields 1 cake.

Frosting:
8 ounces cream cheese
1 stick butter
1 16-ounce box confectioners' sugar

6 ounces chopped pecans

Blend softened cream cheese with the butter until very smooth. Add sugar and continue to blend until smooth. Stir in the pecans. Spread frosting between layers and over the top and side of the cake.

THE SOUTHERN TRACE
Lavonia

THE SOUTHERN TRACE

It was a wispy, warm Indian summer day when I walked through the tall trees that shade the Southern Trace. Entering the 1918 southern mansion, I instantly felt that the first page in a novel of mystery and romance was turning. Letting my fantasy run, I imagined myself the daughter of the house returning home after many months. I marveled at my home's new décor. The parlor was now done in a shade of peach, and the room where I had learned to embroider was decorated in mauve. There were dining tables set with mama's favorite silver plates laid within the larger china ones. And above the mantel hung a portrait of a prize-winning Paso Fino show horse.

Feeling hungry after my long trip, I went to the dining room to find that it, too, was redone in papa's favorite blue. Even the dining room table sported handsome brass plates. I asked for some food and realized my family must have hired a new cook because I couldn't ever remember being served this saucy Cajun Shrimp appetizer or Oysters baked in butter with Parmesan cheese on top and an African daisy to decorate the dish.

No sooner had I washed down these delicacies with a glass of light and springy white wine than a refreshing lime sorbet arrived, set in a scooped-out lemon peel. Mercy me, I thought I would bring the latest fashion home, but what I'd seen in my travels couldn't compare with this. Next, the servant brought me a light, crunchy salad of wilted spinach with bacon, mushrooms and pecans.

I realized with a start that my secret might have been uncovered during my absence, especially with all the redecorating. I had to see what had been done upstairs before eating another bite! Ascending the stairway, I went to the room that had always been called the doll's room. I reached behind the redesigned cornice board—a perfect hiding place—and breathed a sigh of relief. My secret love letters were still there.

Knowing that my forbidden lover was still unknown to my family, my appetite revived. I returned downstairs to partake of a tangy dish of Cuban Pork Sauté, a bit of succulent Islander

Lime Chicken that could replace the fried kind any day, and a wonderful combination of Scallops and Lobster. I hadn't sampled food so delicately seasoned in a long time.

The servant then came with a tray of distinctive desserts. My word, I just had to have a taste of each! The first was an extracreamy Praline Cheesecake; next, a decadently rich Deep Chocolate Mocha Cake with Brandy Icing; and finally, an almost-as-rich Chocolate Mousse with Amaretto. The only dessert I remembered from before my trip was mama's good old Candy Apple Cake. To finish my meal, the servants presented coffee with rainbow sugar crystals and whipped cream.

I felt like a stroll in the garden, but as soon as I stepped outside, I realized that the interlude had come to an end. My fantasy was over, except for the memories that this fantastic restaurant helped me create.

The Southern Trace is located off Highway 17 in Lavonia. Dinner is served from 5:30 p.m. until 10:00 p.m. Tuesday through Saturday. Sunday buffet is available from 11:45 a.m. until 3:00 p.m. For reservations call (404) 356-1033.

THE SOUTHERN TRACE'S CUBAN PORK SAUTE

1½ pounds pork tenderloin
1 teaspoon oregano
½ teaspoon black pepper
⅓ cup chopped onions
4 teaspoons minced garlic
⅓ to ½ cup Italian salad dressing

3 to 4 tablespoons olive oil
3 tablespoons chopped scallions for garnish
1 cup black beans, cooked
1¼ cups white rice, cooked

Cut meat into bite-sized pieces and place in a glass bowl. Sprinkle with oregano and pepper. Add onions and garlic and pour dressing over top. Cover and refrigerate for 24 hours, turning periodically. Heat olive oil in skillet until very hot. Put the entire contents of meat and marinade in skillet and sauté until very brown. Garnish with scallions and serve with beans and rice. Serves 4.

THE SOUTHERN TRACE'S CAJUN SPICY SHRIMP

Cajun Seasoning:
- 1 teaspoon ground red pepper
- 1 teaspoon black pepper
- 1 teaspoon garlic powder
- 1 teaspoon celery seed
- 1 teaspoon commercial creole seasoning mix

Combine all spices in a jar or bag and shake well.

Cajun Sauce:
- 1 large ripe tomato
- 1 12-ounce jar chunky-style hot sauce
- 1 14-ounce can stewed tomatoes
- ½ bell pepper, finely chopped
- ½ medium onion, finely chopped
- 1 tablespoon oregano

Crush tomato in food processor and add remaining ingredients, turning on and off quickly to combine, but not to purée.

- 1 pound fresh shrimp, shelled and deveined (any size)
- 3 tablespoons or more olive oil
- lemon slices for garnish

Dredge shrimp in Cajun Seasoning, coating both sides. Heat olive oil in large skillet until very hot. Add shrimp and sauté about 3 minutes. Lower heat to simmer and ladle about 2 cups of Cajun Sauce over shrimp; simmer for about 10 minutes. Serve with sauce and garnish with lemon slices. Refrigerate remaining sauce for use with other meats and vegetables. Serves 4 to 6.

RUDOLPH'S ON GREEN STREET
Gainesville

RUDOLPH'S ON GREEN STREET

Some of us grew up in English Tudor houses, and some of us only wish we did. Either group would delight in dining at Rudolph's, relishing the ambiance and the food to which we would like to become accustomed. The outside is all wide green lawns and flagged patios. The inside abounds with dark wood and Oriental rugs and has an enviable amount of Duncan Phyfe furniture, not to mention four tile fireplaces. A wraparound porch has been cleverly converted into a dining area and bar that, while maintaining the tone of the place, has enough track lighting and other modern amenities to guarantee it doesn't feel too much like Sunday dinner at Great-aunt Mathilda's.

The service is relaxed and easy, as it should be. You can go there in your elegant best, and if you do, remember to pause and admire yourself in the enormous mirror by the wine cellar. But, if on the other hand you should be on your way to, say, Lake Lanier, and wearing your sailing togs, you would still be welcome and made to feel at home.

At Rudolph's you can have a glass of wine and dine lightly on Pasta or Chicken Salad or, if you're feeling extravagant—and thin—indulge in everything from Onion Soup Gratinée to Chocolate Pecan Pie, at which point you will begin to understand why the women who originally lived in English Tudor houses wore corsets. The Filet au Poivre and Roast Duck are house specialties, but whatever you order, have rolls or muffins. They are scrumptious. There is entertainment on Saturday night and a sedate brunch on Sundays.

If after dining at Rudolph's you should feel overcome with ennui or, more likely, a desire to work off some calories, take a stroll up and down Green Street. The broad, tree-lined street is flanked by historic homes and sweet-smelling gardens. It is one of the loveliest streets you'll ever wander.

Rudolph's on Green Street is located at 700 Green Street in Gainesville. Breakfast is served Monday through Saturday from 10:00 a.m. until 2:30 p.m. and on Sunday from 8:00 a.m.

until 2:30 p.m. Brunch on Sunday is served from 11:00 a.m. until 2:30 p.m. Lunch is served Monday through Saturday from 11:30 a.m. until 2:30 p.m.; dinner is served Monday through Thursday evening from 5:30 until 10:00 and Friday and Saturday evening from 6:00 until 11:00. The lounge opens at 5:00 p.m. For reservations call (404) 534-2226.

RUDOLPH'S ROAST DUCK WITH "SHADOWS OF THE TECHE" SAUCE

4 large ducks
salt and pepper to taste
1 medium onion, peeled
 and quartered
1 apple, cored and
 quartered

1 orange, quartered
2 stalks celery, cut in pieces
¼ cup butter, melted
"Shadows of the Teche"
 Sauce (recipe below)

Dry, then salt and pepper the ducks inside and out. Stuff each cavity with the onion, apple and orange quarters and with pieces of celery. Place in a large roasting pan, leaving space between each duck. Roast at 325 degrees for 15 minutes. Remove excess grease from the pan and baste the ducks with melted butter. Continue basting every 15 minutes during cooking time. (A large duck will be cooked rare in approximately 40 minutes, medium in an hour and well done in 1½ hours. A small duck will be rare in approximately 30 minutes, medium in 40 minutes and well done in 50 minutes.) Glaze ducks with "Shadows of the Teche" Sauce in the final minutes of roasting. Serve with the remaining sauce on the side. Serves 8.

"Shadows of the Teche" Sauce:
⅓ cup orange juice
¼ cup lemon juice
1 cup powdered sugar

2 tablespoons currant jelly
grated rind of 1 lemon
1 tablespoon horseradish

Combine ingredients and mix until smooth, beating well. Heat the sauce over low heat. The sauce may be made the preceding day and kept in the refrigerator. Be sure to bring it to room temperature before heating to serve.

RUDOLPH'S CHOCOLATE PECAN PIE

3 eggs
½ cup sugar
½ stick butter, melted
1 teaspoon vanilla extract
½ cup flour
1¼ cups pecans, chopped
1 cup chocolate minichips
1 9-inch pie shell

Lightly whip the eggs with an electric mixer set on low speed. Add the sugar, melted butter and vanilla, and mix until thoroughly combined. Add flour gradually and mix until blended. Turn the mixer to medium speed and add the pecans and chocolate chips. When blended, pour into an unbaked pie shell and bake in a 350-degree oven for 30 to 45 minutes. Serve warm, with a scoop of vanilla ice cream if desired. Yields 1 pie.

THE WOODBRIDGE INN
Jasper

THE WOODBRIDGE INN

The Woodbridge Inn restaurant was not serving lunch the first day I went by to visit its owners, the Ruefferts. Nevertheless, car after car drove up to the porch where we were sitting. "We drove fifty miles!" people said. "We drove a hundred miles!" Joe Rueffert gave them directions to other eateries nearby.

"What is it about your place?" I said, having heard even in jaded Atlanta that the Woodbridge is very special.

"I buy the best," said Rueffert. "But then a lot of people do that—no shortcuts, all fresh food. But it's no use for me to buy the best ingredients, and prepare them, if the food is not eaten immediately. Food is at its height the moment it comes off the stove. After that . . ." he shrugs. "So I run my restaurant so that when I have a meal prepared and I say 'Pick up!' my waiters run!"

He made it sound so easy, I rhapsodized for days that I had found the secret to a perfect meal—fleet-footed service. Then I remembered that Joe Rueffert had modestly ignored his own European training and expertise. During several visits I had discovered that his best is considerably better than mine. I could roller-skate to the dinner table, and my Rainbow Trout would not be as succulent as his Rainbow Trout. Nor would my Filet Mignon Forestière, Crabmeat Gratinée, Peach Melba or Lemon Cream Pie ever quite match his. Nevertheless, the two recipes which follow have been happily received by my friends and family and will, no doubt, be similarly received by yours. Be advised that though the dishes are called Newberg and Rockefeller, they are not the standard recipes for those dishes. This may be because Joe, himself, doesn't use the recipes anymore. "Oh, no. I just cook it until it's right."

The restaurant itself used to be Ed Lenning's inn. He started it with the proceeds from his gold strike in California and ran it himself for years, taking time out to fight as a Confederate soldier in the Civil War. The hotel served travelers as a stagecoach stop. When the railroad came through Jasper, it passed right in front of the inn, which then became a haven for Floridians eager to escape to the mountains for the summer.

The restaurant is not decorated as a period piece, however. The tone is European. If you ever spent time in the southern Alps or northern Italy and miss the ambiance, you'll love the Woodbridge Inn restaurant. It's clean, green and natural blonde, with homespun tablecloths topped with white linen and flowers. If you arrive before dusk, you can sip your wine and nibble your salad while watching the sun set over the mountains, and you'll understand why the place has lured such a succession of weary travelers to its bed and board.

The Woodbridge Inn is located at 411 Chambers Street in Jasper. The inn's restaurant is open on Tuesday, Wednesday and Thursday from 5:30 p.m. to 9:00 p.m., and on Friday and Saturday from 5:00 p.m to 10:00 p.m. On Sunday it is open for lunch from 11:00 a.m. to 3:00 p.m. For reservations (recommended) call (404) 692-6293.

THE WOODBRIDGE INN'S OYSTERS ROCKEFELLER

10 ounces fresh spinach
2 stalks celery
1 small onion
½ jalapeño pepper
1 clove garlic
2 tablespoons butter
1 tablespoon soy sauce
½ teaspoon garlic salt
½ teaspoon white pepper
dash of Pernod
24 oysters
Hollandaise Sauce (recipe follows)
½ cup Parmesan and Romano cheeses, grated fine

Chop the spinach and cook it in water until tender; then remove from heat and let sit for a few minutes. Mince finely the celery, onion, pepper and garlic; sauté them in butter until soft. Drain the spinach and add it to the celery mix. Stir in the soy sauce, garlic salt, white pepper and a dash of Pernod.
Shuck the oysters and place them, on the half-shell, in a casserole or baking pan. Put them in a 350-degree oven until the shells are hot. Then put a spoonful of the spinach mixture on each oyster, top with Hollandaise Sauce and sprinkle with Parmesan and Romano cheeses. Place oysters under the broiler until brown. Serves 6 as an appetizer.

THE WOODBRIDGE INN'S HOLLANDAISE SAUCE

1 stick butter
1 egg yolk
1 tablespoon boiling water
1 tablespoon lemon juice
dash of cayenne pepper
dash of salt

Melt the butter. Put one egg yolk into a blender and, while blending slowly, add the boiling water and lemon juice. Then pour in the melted butter in a thin, continuous stream. Add cayenne pepper and salt to taste. Yields ¾ cup.

THE WOODBRIDGE INN'S SEAFOOD A LA NEWBERG

1 stick butter
6 tablespoons flour
1½ cups chicken broth
¼ cup dry sherry
4 tablespoons Hungarian paprika
2 stalks celery, diced
1 onion, diced
1 clove garlic, diced
1 jalapeño pepper, diced (no seeds)
½ pound shrimp, peeled and deveined
½ pound scallops
¼ pound crabmeat, picked
2 ounces cognac
1 cup grated cheeses (mix of mozzarella, mild Cheddar and Swiss)

Make a roux by melting 5 tablespoons of the butter and adding the flour, stirring over low heat for a few minutes until honey-colored. Add the chicken stock, stirring continuously until thickened. Add sherry and paprika and let simmer.

Put half the remaining butter in a frying pan and sauté the celery, onion, garlic and jalapeño pepper until glazed. Add the mixture to the thickened stock. Then sauté the seafood in the rest of the butter until the shrimp turns pink, and add it to the stock, along with the cognac. Pour the mixture into a casserole or individual ramekins, and top with cheese. Broil until the cheese bubbles and browns. Serves 2 to 4.

THE TATE HOUSE
Tate

THE TATE HOUSE

Marble has long been an architectural symbol of wealth and durability, and of the people who could afford to put bits of it in their homes, as fireplaces or desk tops or pastry boards. Like a diamond, marble somehow transcends itself and becomes more than just a piece of mottled rock. No one knew that better than Colonel Samuel Tate, president of the Georgia Marble Company, and in the 1920s he began to build himself a house of it—a whole house of Etowah pink marble. The eldest of nineteen children, Colonel Tate never married, and he lived in his marble house with his sister and brother until he died.

The Tate House is an amazing place. It was fashionable in the '20s to build homes that presented a different face on each side to suit the varying moods of their occupants. The Tate House presents on its front a classical, columned, southern mansion. But walk through the formal gardens that surround the house and you'll find yourself looking alternately at a Mediterranean villa, an Italianate residence or a London club. Inside, the place has been meticulously restored—here a Chippendale-furnished parlor, there a walnut-paneled board room—and you can feel free to wander around for a while if you like. Then it's time to pull yourself together, perhaps have a drink, and eat.

In the pub downstairs, formerly the garage, you can cozy up to the bar, a lovely thing which has been imported from a Belgian castle. Next, you can retire to one of the dining rooms, or you can have a drink and dinner in glassed-in splendor in the greenhouse and enjoy the panorama of gardens, marble walks, statuary and fountains spread out before you.

The menu changes weekly. You can brunch on a fresh fruit cup or try the Seafood Gumbo and Poached Eggs Brennan. For dinner you could choose an appetizer of Shrimp Cocktail with Sauce Elizabeth or Marinated Mushrooms and Artichoke Hearts, procede to the Tate Mansion Salad, then on to Roast Rack of Lamb with Mint Sauce and, finally, to Bourbon Pie or one of the Tate House's other tantalizing desserts.

Sam Tate started building his house when he was in his sixties, and its design and placement reflect both a mature man's wisdom and an energetic man's dream—not to mention a rich man's money. As a way to use marble, the Tate House has tombstones beat coming and going.

The Tate House is on Highway 53 in Tate. The restaurant is open for lunch and dinner Wednesday through Saturday, and for brunch on Sunday. The hours vary with the season. For more information or reservations call (800) 342-7515 in Georgia (toll-free); outside Georgia call (404) 735-3122.

THE TATE HOUSE'S SWEET GEORGIA BREAD

1 cup grits, cooked
2 tablespoons butter
1 cup cornmeal
1 teaspoon cinnamon
¼ teaspoon nutmeg
¾ cup chopped pecans or walnuts
¾ cup brown sugar
1 cup milk

Stir together the warm, cooked grits and the butter until the butter melts. Add the remaining ingredients in the order listed above. Pour mixture into a greased loafpan and bake at 400 degrees for 25 to 30 minutes or until done. The bread will be flat and crumbly, with a consistency like cornbread. Yields 1 loaf.

THE TATE HOUSE'S SADDLE OF BEEF FIORENTINE

1 15-pound boned strip loin
4 onions
3 stalks celery
2 bunches parsley
6 pieces garlic
2 leeks
4 ounces brandy
4 ounces Madeira wine
4 ounces olive oil
2 ounces crushed peppercorns
1 tablespoon thyme
1 tablespoon oregano

Separate the fat from the loin meat and peel it away, down to the last inch on the small side of the meat, but leave it attached. Finely chop the onions, celery, parsley, garlic and leeks, and combine with the brandy, Madeira, oil and spices to make the marinade. Place half of this mixture between the fat and the lean meat. Turn the loin over and place the remaining marinade on the bottom, meaty side. Cover and marinate in the refrigerator for three days. Remove all marinade and brown the beef in the broiler. Bake at 350 degrees for 35 to 40 minutes. Remove from heat and set aside for 30 minutes to draw the juices into the meat. Serves 20.

THE OLD MILL RESTAURANT
Cedartown

THE OLD MILL RESTAURANT

On your way to the Old Mill Restaurant, tell your children or companions a story about how life used to be lived in northwest Georgia in the 1800s. Most people in Cedar Valley lived on farms in the hills and hollows, and they ate what they grew and sold what was left over. By 1848 there were enough farms to justify a mill, so Asa Prior charged a slave, Milton Hanie, with the task of building one on Big Cedar Creek that could grind both wheat and corn. Families would hitch up their wagons on a sunny Saturday and drive to the mill with their harvested corn and wheat, and probably a picnic basket and fishing poles as well, for going to the mill was an all-day affair. A farmer would leave a number of bushels in the morning and get, that afternoon, his measure back, less the percentage the miller kept for his trouble. The miller sold his allotment in town to city dwellers. While the family waited, they would eat, fish in the inviting spot made by the dam and visit with other folks doing the same thing. What they went home with would help feed them until the next crops were harvested.

When you get to the Old Mill, a bowl of homemade Vegetable Soup and a pone of Cornbread will be rushed immediately to your table, so that you can sustain yourself while waiting for dinner. You might want a dozen Apalachicola Bay Oysters on the Half-shell to begin with. Then, if beef is your preference, order a steak that is freshly cut in the kitchen and broiled over hickory charcoal. The fish is also fresh and can be had either fried or grilled. Vegetable dishes include Squash Casserole and Corn Pudding; both are hearty and filling.

If you can spare a minute from the country feast before you, pause and look about you. The restoration of the Old Mill began in 1959, fourteen years after it closed as a mill. Now Hunter P. Stephens, son of the restorers, carries on the tradition. The fireplace of native stone dominating the north wall will hold a six-foot log. It was added when the Stephenses closed up the loading dock used by wagons. The brick floor was added too; the original was dirt. And of course the lovely, sunny, glassed-in patio cantilevered out over the mill trace is an addition. You can sit there nibbling trout in air-conditioned comfort and drink a toast to Old Allen, the slave who was the first miller. He never had it so good.

If Stephens is around, ask him to turn on the wheel for you. He keeps it in working order. As the cogs turn and the first gallons of water gush down across the blades, the whole building trembles slightly; the wheel shudders, begins to groan and turns. There is a deep, wonderful roar. Stephens leans out the window and smiles, communing with his mill. You get the feeling that wherever Old Allen is, he's smiling too.

The Old Mill Restaurant is located on Highway 27 South in Cedartown. It is open for dinner Thursday through Sunday from 5:00 p.m. until 10:30 p.m. For reservations call (404) 748-2531.

THE OLD MILL RESTAURANT'S CORN PUDDING

2 eggs
2 cups grated fresh corn (or 2 packages frozen cream corn, prepared according to package directions)
1 tablespoon sugar
1½ cups scalded milk
1 teaspoon salt
3 tablespoons melted butter

Beat eggs slightly and mix with all other ingredients. Pour corn mixture into a buttered casserole and cook very slowly for 1 to 1½ hours at 300 degrees. Serves 4.

THE OLD MILL RESTAURANT'S CORNBREAD

2½ cups self-rising cornmeal
½ cup self-rising flour
¼ teaspoon baking soda
1 tablespoon sugar
1 egg, slightly beaten
1¼ cups buttermilk
3 tablespoons bacon drippings

Mix the dry ingredients and add the egg and buttermilk. Beat well. Heat the bacon drippings in a 9-inch iron skillet and pour the drippings into the cornbread mixture, mixing well. Pour the mixture into the skillet and bake at 425 degrees for 20 to 25 minutes. Serves 6 to 8.

THE OLD MILL RESTAURANT'S SQUASH CASSEROLE

2 cups cooked, mashed squash
¼ cup chopped onions
½ cup grated Cheddar cheese
1 teaspoon salt
1 teaspoon pepper
1 tablespoon cornstarch
½ cup milk
¼ cup melted butter
2 eggs, well beaten

To the squash, add the onions, cheese, salt, pepper, cornstarch and milk. Mix well, then stir in the butter and eggs. Place in a well-greased casserole and bake at 325 degrees for 45 minutes to an hour. Serves 4.

LICKSKILLET FARM
Alpharetta

LICKSKILLET FARM

One of the charms of the Atlanta suburbs is that there are little country enclaves flourishing among them. One minute you're surrounded by discount stores and miles of pavement, but turn one corner, go around a bend and voilà! You're greeted by rolling hills sprinkled with trees, watered by a meandering brook and here and there dotted with cows. In such a niche is Lickskillet Farm, complete with a Civil War entrenchment in the back yard, down by Foekiller Creek. The old Miller farmhouse, which had stood vacant for years, was gently restored in the 1950s to a level of comfort and elegance its original owners probably never knew. Better us than them. From the hunter-green walls and the peach-colored napkins to the Helen Means pictures on the walls, Lickskillet's version of Country is very elegant indeed.

If you can tear your eyes away from the pastoral setting or the pictures to glance briefly at the menu, you will see a dozen or so entrées, among them Scallops Mornay au Gratin, Fried Chicken Country Elegance and Alaskan King Crab Legs. Pick one, and a four-course dinner automatically follows—soup with cracklin' cornbread, salad, two hot and two cold vegetables and dessert. And every dinner is completed with homemade Gingerbread with Whiskey Sauce. You are thus spared adding up a damage estimate in your head as you go. You are also spared being accused of gluttony. Dessert is, after all, already paid for. You can select wine by wandering into the cellar yourself. Children are not only welcome, their meals are half-price. For entertainment, there's always Uncle Bill, who has been playing his grand piano by the fireplace for twelve years.

On Sundays, Lickskillet Farm offers a champagne brunch of fruits, eggs, grits, hot and cold meats, homemade breads and, of course, champagne.

The charm of the place, besides the country food, which is undeniably good, is that you feel that dining at home ought to be like this. And it would be, too, if only you had the time. And the piano. And a wine cellar. And Uncle Bill.

Lickskillet Farm is located on Old Roswell Road in Alpharetta. It is open for dinner Tuesday through Saturday from 6:30 p.m. until 10:00 p.m.; and Sunday brunch is served from 11:30 a.m. until 2:15 p.m. For reservations (recommended) call (404) 475-6484.

LICKSKILLET FARM'S
CHICKEN BREASTS IN WINE

4 chicken breasts
salt and white pepper to taste
garlic powder to taste
2 tablespoons butter
2 tablespoons oil

½ cup chicken bouillon
½ cup wine
2 tablespoons butter
2 tablespoons flour
2 cups sautéed mushrooms

Sprinkle the chicken breasts with salt, pepper and garlic powder, and sauté them in a mixture of butter and oil until browned on all sides. Add the chicken bouillon and the wine to the chicken and simmer, covered, for about 20 minutes or until the chicken is done. Meanwhile, prepare a roux in another pan by melting two tablespoons butter and adding two tablespoons flour, stirring gently with a fork until light brown. When the chicken is done, remove it to a platter and thicken the sauce left in the skillet by stirring the roux into the pan juice, whisking over low heat until thickened. (If too much liquid has boiled out of the pan, it may be necessary to add more and heat it before thickening.) When the sauce is ready, pour it over the chicken and top with mushrooms. Serve with rice pilaf if desired. Serves 4.

LICKSKILLET FARM'S CHICKEN LIVERS

12 to 16 chicken livers, membranes removed
salt, pepper and Accent to taste
flour for dusting
2 tablespoons butter or margarine

1 tablespoon minced onions
1 cup sliced fresh mushrooms

Sprinkle the livers with salt, pepper and Accent; dust them lightly with flour. Sauté livers briefly in butter or margarine until brown, then add minced onions and mushrooms. Cover and simmer for 5 to 10 minutes, allowing the vegetables to cook. Serve with rice pilaf if desired. Serves 2.

LICKSKILLET FARM'S GINGERBREAD WITH WHISKEY SAUCE

Gingerbread:
- **1 cup water**
- **1 cup melted shortening**
- **1 cup sugar**
- **1 cup molasses**
- **3 eggs, well beaten**
- **3 cups plain flour**
- **1 teaspoon baking powder**
- **1 teaspoon baking soda**
- **1½ teaspoons ginger**
- **1 teaspoon salt**
- **1½ teaspoons cinnamon**

Boil the water and pour it over the shortening, then add the sugar, molasses and beaten eggs. In another bowl sift together the flour, baking powder, soda, ginger, salt and cinnamon. Add the dry ingredients to the liquid, and beat the mixture with an egg beater until smooth. Pour the batter into a well-greased 13-by-9-by-3-inch loafpan. Bake in a preheated 350-degree oven for 25 to 35 minutes until set. Let the bread cool on a rack and serve it with hot Whiskey Sauce. Serves 8.

Whiskey Sauce:
- **2 cups water**
- **1 cup sugar**
- **¼ teaspoon salt**
- **2 tablespoons butter**
- **½ teaspoon nutmeg**
- **2½ tablespoons cornstarch**
- **¼ cup whiskey (bourbon)**

Boil the water in a saucepan and mix in the sugar, salt, butter and nutmeg; bring to a second boil. Dissolve the cornstarch in a little water and add it and the whiskey to the mixture, stirring until it is slightly thickened. Serve hot.

THE PUBLIC HOUSE ON ROSWELL SQUARE
Roswell

THE PUBLIC HOUSE ON ROSWELL SQUARE

Creek Indians lived in the Chattahoochee River basin one hundred and fifty years ago. They fished and hunted and chased off a few trespassing settlers, for which crime they were invited to resettle several states westward. Then in 1837 Roswell King and friends came to the Chattahoochee basin and built a series of cotton mills and a little town named, appropriately enough, Roswell. It was a charming place, boasting among other things a company store in which employees of the mills could purchase goods on credit. Everything was sold in such stores—food, hardware, wood, cloth, even coffins. In the Roswell Company Store you could even get your teeth pulled. Today, the same building houses something a good deal more pleasant than a dentist's office—the Public House on Roswell Square. For thirteen years now, this restaurant has been a source of joy and succor to its many friends.

Some people will only visit the Public House at night because they like to go upstairs and sit at the bar, soaking up the atmosphere of pub life which predominates there. Others maintain that lunch time is when the place is its most delightful. I vote for rainy Saturdays, myself. Its red-and-white striped awnings are easy to spot in a downpour, and there is a cozy entrance in which to shake off your umbrella. The glossy white plaster and rough brick walls, crisp linen tablecloths, willowware and fresh flowers make you feel less wet and frazzled and more welcome.

The food at the Public House makes you feel welcome too. My husband ordered the Garden Frittata, an omelet topped with potatoes, tomatoes and a sour cream and chive sauce. I compromised on a Hamburger, Marinated Chicken Livers and a side order of Zucchini. Then I had the Amaretto Ice Cream Torte. In a place with track lighting, you can get away with such shenanigans.

After lunch, which was perfect, I sneaked up the stairs to the then-deserted pub room, hoping to see the resident ghost. I was disappointed. He is Thaddeus, a Confederate veteran who reportedly died here during the Civil War when the building served a stint as a field hospital before returning to civilian life as a general store. All offers to have him exorcised have been refused by the management, who feel that they are comfortable with Thaddeus if Thaddeus is comfortable with them. He could do a lot worse.

The Public House on Roswell Square is located at 605 South Atlantic Street in Roswell. It is open for lunch from 11:30 a.m. until 2:30 p.m. Monday through Friday, and from 11:30 a.m. until 3:00 p.m. on Saturday. Dinner hours are from 5:30 p.m. until 10:00 p.m. Monday through Thursday, and from 5:30 p.m. until 11:00 p.m. on Friday and Saturday. The Public House does not take reservations, but for information call (404) 992- 4646.

THE PUBLIC HOUSE'S
MARINATED CHICKEN LIVERS

Marinade:
2 tablespoons apple cider vinegar
2 tablespoons lemon juice
1 teaspoon garlic salt
½ teaspoon white pepper
½ teaspoon dry mustard
1 cup vegetable oil

To prepare the marinade, combine all ingredients except oil in a blender or food processor and blend for 30 seconds. Gradually add the oil in a stream and blend until smooth. Set aside.

Liver:
½ cup flour
1½ teaspoons salt
½ teaspoon pepper
2 pints chicken livers
2 tablespoons oil
2 green peppers
leaf lettuce
18 cherry tomatoes for garnish

Mix a handful of flour, the salt and the pepper in a shallow bowl and dredge the livers in it until coated. Heat the oil in a frying pan over medium heat and sauté the livers a few at a time until they stiffen. Turn them over and continue to cook about two minutes until firm but still pink inside. Remove from heat. Julienne the green peppers and combine them with the livers in a glass bowl. Add the marinade and refrigerate several hours or overnight. To serve, drain the marinade and place the livers and peppers on leaf lettuce and garnish with 3 cherry tomatoes per serving. Serves 4 to 6.

THE PUBLIC HOUSE'S
AMARETTO ICE CREAM TORTE

2 10-inch chocolate chip cookies
1 cup semisweet chocolate syrup
½ gallon amaretto ice cream
1 cup toasted slivered almonds
5 cups whipped cream

Place one cookie in the bottom of a 10-inch springform pan, trimming it if necessary to make it fit. Spread half the syrup on top of the cookie, and spread the softened ice cream on top of that. Add the rest of the syrup, and top with the other cookie, again trimming if necessary. Cover with plastic wrap and freeze overnight. When ready to serve, remove the sides of the springform pan, and press almonds into the edges of the torte. To serve, cut torte into tenths. Top each serving with whipped cream. Serves 10.

MAXIMILLIAN'S
Marietta

MAXIMILLIAN'S

Next time you find yourself negotiating I–75 during rush hour in Atlanta, spare a millisecond to glance northwest, and contemplate. In the late 1920s a Marietta lawyer built himself a hunting lodge a few miles north of you. His name was James Carmichael, and he owned much of the land thereabouts and wanted a quiet retreat from which to sally forth into the woods with his guns on crisp autumn mornings. (The woods are part of what we now know as Lockheed and Dobbins Air Force Base.) Carmichael liked his little place so well that he finally moved into it full time, adding along the way a swimming pool and electricity—the first of either to grace a private residence in Cobb County.

The hunting lodge is now a restaurant called Maximillian's. It looks like a mountain house, all shingles and stone, tucked into the side of a hill. A series of small, paneled rooms follow each other in comfortable succession; the atmosphere is intimate and secluded. There's a large stone fireplace, which on chilly days will have a fire in it. Downstairs is the stone-floored bar and a lounge overlooking the pool, now a home for ducks. The pool isn't like the ones built these days. It's a cement pond, sort of, built as a holding pool for a stream in those old days before chlorination. I have always wanted to swim in an old-fashioned pool like this, and someday I might just drink too many Pink Carlottas and give those complacent ducks a run for their money.

Meanwhile, I can easily content myself with Teriyaki Tenderloin Tips, Soft-shell Crabs, Steak au Poivre or Veal a la Oscar—whatever the waiter recommends. It's all good. Maximillian's makes you feel very agreeable. No wonder Carmichael liked it so much.

Maximillian's is located at 1857 Airport Industrial Park Avenue in Marietta. It is open for lunch Tuesday through Friday from 11:30 a.m. until 2:00 p.m. Dinner is served from 6:00 p.m.

to 10:00 p.m. Monday through Thursday and from 6:00 p.m. to 11:00 p.m. on Friday and Saturday. Reservations are recommended; call (404) 955-4286.

MAXIMILLIAN'S STUFFED FLOUNDER

6 8-ounce flounder fillets
salt and pepper to taste
Crabmeat Stuffing (recipe follows)

1 cup Hollandaise Sauce (see Index)

Salt and pepper the fillets and spoon one-sixth of the stuffing onto the center of each one. Fold the ends of each fillet over and place them in a baking dish. Bake at 325 degrees until creamy white, about 15 or 20 minutes. Top each fillet with Hollandaise Sauce before serving. Serves 6.

Crabmeat Stuffing:
1 egg
1 tablespoon half-and-half
2 tablespoons mayonnaise
½ teaspoon Old Bay Seasoning (or crab boil)
½ tablespoon Worcestershire sauce
½ teaspoon white pepper
½ teaspoon salt

1½ tablespoons pimiento
2 tablespoons parsley flakes
2 tablespoons finely chopped onions
2 tablespoons finely chopped green peppers
1 pound blue crabmeat

Mix all the ingredients well, adding the crabmeat last.

Note: This can be used to stuff fish or avocados.

MAXIMILLIAN'S PINK CARLOTTA

1½ ounces rum
1½ ounces peach brandy
6 to 8 ounces pineapple juice

orange slice for garnish
maraschino cherry for garnish

Blend in a shaker the rum, brandy and juice. Pour over ice and garnish with an orange slice and a cherry. Serves 1.

MAXIMILLIAN'S
CARROTS AU GRAND MARNIER

1 ½ pounds carrots
2 cups orange juice
1 cup brown sugar
1 ounce Grand Marnier

Peel and slice the carrots, and parboil them until tender. Stir together the orange juice, brown sugar and Grand Marnier, then add the drained carrots to the mix. Marinate in the refrigerator for 24 hours, and reheat the carrots in their marinade to serve. Serves 4 to 6.

MAXIMILLIAN'S
CREAM OF MUSHROOM SOUP

1 pound fresh mushrooms, sliced
4 cups water
4 cups heavy cream
1½ cups sherry (or less, to taste)
½ teaspoon white pepper
4 tablespoons chicken base or bouillon
1½ sticks butter
6 tablespoons flour

Cook the mushrooms in the water until tender. Add the cream, sherry, pepper and chicken base and bring to a boil. Meanwhile, make the roux in a sauté pan by melting the butter and stirring into it 6 tablespoons flour. Cook, stirring, until the flour has cooked and turned light brown. Add the roux to the boiling soup a little at a time, adding only what is necessary to thicken the soup to your taste. Serves 4.

THE PLANTERS RESTAURANT
Marietta

THE PLANTERS RESTAURANT

In the South, as elsewhere, an important social game is "Who do you know?" In Georgia during the summer of 1864, it became more than a game—people played seriously and for keeps, using real bullets. The person to know was General William Tecumseh Sherman or, as he was more familiarly known, that Yankee Pyromaniac. The rules were simple: If you had ever known General Sherman in school or in the army, or if you knew any of his family, or if you knew anyone who knew any of his family, it was to your enormous advantage to run out into the front yard at the first sign of a bluecoat and yell, "Ya'll know where I can find Cousin Sherman, honey?" Prompt action along those lines might not save your silver, but it could leave a roof over your head.

Fortunately for posterity, the general did seem to have at least a nodding acquaintance with a good many southerners, among them William King, whose wife owned Bushy Park, a three-thousand-acre plantation outside Marietta. King was able to negotiate to save their seventeen-room Greek Revival home from the torch, though it got shot up a bit and emptied of all its furniture. Having survived that set-to with admirable aplomb, the house settled into a comfortable middle age in the early twentieth century as the home of the Garrison family. There were seventeen Garrison children, but any house that could make it through a war could make it through seventeen children.

Now it's the Planters Restaurant, genteel, old and fine as Limoges, all decked out for company in Victorian finery and Oriental rugs. It is the archetypal midnineteenth-century southern house, with wide central halls upstairs and down, miles of wainscotting and front and back stairs. The bar-lounge at the back of the house is where the back porch used to be. Upstairs are two rooms preserved with Victorian furnishings.

When you're through gawking, you can eat, thus receiving two treats for the price of one. Dinner at the Planters is a five-course affair. For twenty to thirty dollars, not counting wine, you will dine on something like Veal Terrine with Tomato Chutney and Lemon-Hazelnut Dressing, Gin and Tomato Soup, a Spinach and Citrus Salad, Roast Prime Rib and Strawberry Charlotte. And over dessert you can gaze out at the rose garden or the stars twinkling through the magnolias, and thank God that, unlike the women who used to grace these hallowed halls, you don't have to worry about an eighteen-inch waist.

The Planters Restaurant is located at 780 South Cobb Drive in Marietta. It opens for dinner Monday through Thursday at 6:30 p.m., and Friday and Saturday at 6:00 p.m. For reservations (recommended) call (404) 427-4646.

THE PLANTERS RESTAURANT'S GROUPER WITH YELLOW PEPPER PUREE

1 yellow bell pepper, roasted, peeled and seeded
12 ounces jumbo lump crabmeat, picked for shells
1 small clove garlic
1 cup heavy cream
½ teaspoon lemon juice
1 tablespoon white wine
2 tablespoons butter, softened
salt to taste
white pepper to taste
2½ pounds grouper fillets, cut into 6 7-ounce pieces
1 cup flour
4 green onions, diced

Purée the peppers, 4 ounces of the crabmeat and the garlic in a food processor. In a saucepan over medium heat, reduce the cream by half. Add the purée, lemon juice and white wine. Bring to a soft boil and slowly add butter, whipping until well blended. Adjust seasoning. Keep sauce warm.

Lightly salt and pepper the grouper, then dust with flour. Sauté in lightly oiled, heated sauté pan until grouper is flakey but firm. Place on plates that you have covered with sauce. Sauté green onions in sauté pan, then add remaining crabmeat. Pour warmed onions and crabmeat over grouper. Serves 6.

THE PLANTERS RESTAURANT'S GIN AND TOMATO SOUP

21 ounces whole canned tomatoes
10 ounces tomato sauce
scant tablespoon paprika
scant ½ teaspoon thyme
¼ teaspoon salt (or to taste)
1½ tablespoons sugar
¼ teaspoon black pepper
scant teaspoon chopped garlic
5 ounces gin (10 tablespoons)
6 or more tablespoons heavy cream
5 ounces bacon, cooked, drained and chopped
3 to 4 ounces shitake mushrooms, julienned and sautéed
3 tablespoons butter, softened

Combine tomatoes, tomato sauce, paprika, thyme, salt, sugar, pepper and garlic in large saucepan and bring to a boil. Reduce heat and simmer 1 to 1½ hours. Add gin and cook another 30 minutes. Add cream and blend; then strain. Add bacon, mushrooms and butter; stir well and serve. (If the soup needs reheating, don't let it boil again.) This soup looks very dramatic served in a hollow yellow bell pepper with the top cut off. The yellow pepper also adds another flavor. Serves 4.

THE MANSION
Atlanta

THE MANSION

By the 1880s Atlanta had recovered somewhat from the unpleasantness with Sherman's army and was undergoing a building boom to reflect its new status as the state capital. Philadelphia railroad man Richard Peters was building too. He liked the area where Ponce de Leon Avenue is today. It was all a forest then, and he thought the wood would make nice fuel for his flour mill. So he bought four hundred acres of it for five dollars an acre. The Peters family later built a mansion in the middle of it—a high Victorian, shingle-style house which reflects, architecturally, the family's Philadelphia heritage. It's enormous, rambling, loaded with charming nooks and crannies.

The Victorians knew a lot about using contrasts of texture and color to add drama to a house, and the Mansion provides a short course in the technique. Where dark wood can lead up to a sparkling leaded-glass window, it does. Where a hall can turn unexpectedly into an opportunity for a tête-à-tête, it will. There are eleven dining rooms in all, and each is completely different from the next. The whole atmosphere is unexpectedly rich and festive. The lobby and the spacious gazebo, a bar featuring nightly entertainment, are recent additions, serene and airy. The courtyard, a dining area which overlooks a lovely fountain, emits just the right amount of careless elegance. On spring Saturdays you are likely to glimpse a wedding out there.

The Mansion's new European-trained chef innovatively combines Old World and American Southern cuisine. You can savor his Grilled Shrimp Cocktail with a Mustard Sauce, Boneless Broiled Duck with Beans or the extraordinary Chocolate Pâté, which won the 1987 "Best Dessert in Atlanta" award. We got the recipe for you. The Oriental Chicken Salad, which we also have the recipe for, looks truly sophisticated, but it brings out the worst in people. I had to slap my cousin's hand three times to keep her fingers out of mine.

If, while paying your bill in the atrium, you hear an unearthly scream in the wall behind the cash register, don't assume it's a fellow diner being tortured for his charge-card number. It's the parrot, getting acquainted with one of the guests. You'll want to get acquainted with the Mansion—and perhaps with its resident parrot—the next time you're in Atlanta.

The Mansion is located at 179 Ponce de Leon Avenue in Atlanta. Lunch is served from 11:30 a.m. to 2:30 p.m. Monday through Friday; brunch is served during the same hours on Saturday and Sunday. Dinner is served from 6:00 p.m. to 11:00 p.m. every day. Reservations are recommended; call (404) 876-0727.

THE MANSION'S ORIENTAL CHICKEN SALAD

4 whole chicken breasts
3 or 4 raw carrots
1 green pepper
1 red bell pepper
2 cups snow peas
1 cup water chestnuts
Miso Dressing (recipe follows)
lettuce leaves
tofu for garnish

Grill the chicken breasts and set them aside to cool. Peel and julienne the carrots and slice the peppers and snow peas. Blanch the vegetables for 30 seconds in boiling water and set aside. Slice the water chestnuts and set them aside. Pull the chicken apart into bite-sized pieces, and combine it with the vegetables. Toss with the Miso Dressing and chill. Serve on lettuce leaves, garnished with tofu. Serves 4 to 6.

Miso Dressing:
½ cup teriyaki sauce
¾ cup white wine
1 tablespoon olive oil
1 bay leaf
dash of salt and pepper
dash of garlic
1 teaspoon fresh ginger (or ½ teaspoon dried ginger)

Mix all the ingredients together and refrigerate overnight. Remove bay leaf before serving.

THE MANSION'S CHOCOLATE PATE

1 pound bittersweet chocolate (Eidelweiss or Lindt, not baking chocolate)
1½ cups brandy
3 to 4 sticks butter
¼ pound white chocolate (Eidelweiss or Lindt)
⅛ cup water
½ pound pecans
15 egg yolks
¼ cup mint jelly

In a double boiler over simmering water melt the bittersweet chocolate with 1 cup brandy and ¾ pound butter. If it seems too thick, add a little more butter. Remove from heat and let cool to room temperature. Also in a double boiler over simmering heat, melt the white chocolate with ½ cup brandy and a couple of tablespoons of water. If the white chocolate needs to be thinned, add a little more water. (It should be relatively thick.) Remove from heat and let cool to room temperature.

Grind the pecans very fine. In a separate bowl, stir the 15 egg yolks. Whip the pecans and the egg yolks into the dark chocolate (not the white chocolate). Oil a bread loafpan well and pour half the dark chocolate into it. Make a channel with a spoon down the middle of the chocolate without touching either end of the pan. Pour the white chocolate into this channel. Ladle a stream of mint jelly on top of the white chocolate, and cover it with the rest of the dark chocolate. Allow the chocolate to chill in the refrigerator for 2 to 4 hours, then fold it out of the mold. To serve, slice the chocolate (as if you're slicing a loaf of bread) and lay it in a dessert plate with fresh fruit or, if desired, top with whipped cream. Serves 8.

Note: Chef Victor Saarela won the "Best Dessert in Atlanta" award for 1987 with this creation.

ANTHONY'S PLANTATION RESTAURANT
Atlanta

ANTHONY'S PLANTATION RESTAURANT

Atlantans, when queried by out-of-towners about a good place to eat, tend to shrug and mutter defensively that it all depends. That's because there are several hundred restaurants in Atlanta, and it really does depend. If you press them, however, if you say, "I want an Old South experience. I want history, good food and lush surroundings, and I don't mind paying for them," they will probably mention Anthony's.

When you see the lovely old 1797 plantation house, tucked up and out of sight behind a doctor's office, you won't believe it's been there for nearly two hundred years. And it hasn't. For most of its life it stood in Washington, Georgia, as the home of the Pope-Walton family, until it was dismantled and moved, brick by painstaking brick, to its present site. It's a plain-styled plantation house; the two central halls, downstairs and upstairs, were originally open walk-throughs providing crossventilation and a wonderful place to get out of the sun on hot afternoons. Nowadays all is enclosed and air-conditioned, but the feel of early nineteenth-century southern life is unmistakable. The old kitchen is all brick, complete with fireplace and ancient cooking paraphenalia. The front rooms are loaded with Chippendale, country English pieces and some finely drawn oil paintings. Behind the bar is the old stone-floored wine cellar, where a group may dine in privacy. My personal favorite is the upstairs porch, where I can look out over the grounds and pretend to be master of all I survey.

Dining is table d'hôte; you can choose a complete, four-course Plantation Harvest Dinner for a set price, or smaller versions for less, including a vegetarian and a grazing option. How about fresh Asparagus on a Rice Cake or fresh Crawfish Tails to start? The Châteaubriand is excellent, or you might try duck any one of five or six ways, or the Spa Cuisine—a healthful, salt-free concoction of veal or fish seasoned with herbs. Dare I mention the Bananas Foster, Key Lime Pie and Chocolate Mousse with Raspberry Sauce?

And if you have cab fare home, try a Frankly My Dear, a heady blend of brandy, rum, Southern Comfort, orange juice and champagne. If Scarlett had had the good sense to offer Rhett one of these on his way out the door, he'd probably still be there, fumbling for his coat.

Anthony's Plantation Restaurant is located at 3109 Piedmont Road in Atlanta. It is open for dinner Monday through Saturday from 6:00 p.m. until everyone has been served. Reservations are recommended; call (404) 262-7379.

ANTHONY'S PLANTATION RESTAURANT'S LOBSTER CHOWDER

2 red bell peppers, finely diced
2 red onions, thinly sliced
2 tablespoons butter
1 cucumber peeled, seeded and diced
1½ pounds steamed lobster, out of shell
2 large prawns (about 2 ounces of shrimp)
6 crawfish, tail meat only
dash of minced chives
dash of saffron
dash of white pepper
dash of black pepper
4 teaspoons Seafood Seasoning (recipe follows)
2 cups whipping cream
3 pounds diced potatoes, boiled
steamed seaweed or steamed spinach

Sauté the bell peppers and onions in butter, adding the cucumber, lobster, shrimp, crawfish and seasonings. Add the cream and simmer until reduced. Add the cooked potatoes and heat, correcting the seasonings. (Sherry or brandy may be added if desired.) Serve over seaweed or spinach. The chowder will be more creamy than liquid and should be served on a plate rather than in a bowl. Serves 4.

Seafood Seasoning:
¼ teaspoon coriander
2 teaspoons Hungarian pepper
½ teaspoon garlic
½ teaspoon cayenne pepper
¾ teaspoon salt

Mix all the spices and herbs together. Yields 4 teaspoons.

ANTHONY'S PLANTATION RESTAURANT'S
BLACK PASTA WITH GOAT CHEESE

1 spaghetti squash
12 ounces black fettucini pasta
1 cup diced Smithfield ham
1 cup black olives, sliced
4 ounces shitake mushrooms
1 red bell pepper, diced
pinches of chopped fresh basil, oregano and cilantro
½ cup garlic butter
8 ounces goat cheese
curly endive for garnish

Split the spaghetti squash and take out the seeds; then steam it until tender. Prepare the pasta according to package directions, or blanch it in boiling water until soft. Drain. While the squash and pasta are cooking, prepare a sauce by sautéing the ham, olives, mushrooms, bell pepper and herbs in the garlic butter. When everything is done, place the pasta on ovenproof plates and surround it with a ring of spaghetti squash, which may be lifted from its peeling with a fork. Spoon the ham-mushroom sauce over the pasta, and cover it with bits of goat cheese. Put the plates under the broiler until the cheese begins to melt and turn brown—a few seconds. Then garnish by placing curly endive between the pasta and the squash. Serves 2.

HERREN'S AND GUIDO'S
Atlanta

HERREN'S AND GUIDO'S

The story of Herren's and Guido's should be a movie. The film opens with a young, redheaded prizefighter, Charlie Herren, walking down Peachtree Street in Atlanta. It is 1934, the middle of the Great Depression, but Charlie has a few dollars in his pocket and is looking for a little place to start a downtown restaurant. He turns down a side street, sees an old building for sale. Looking up, he notices the sign at the corner—Luckie Street. "I found it!" he shouts, throwing his cap into the air. Fadeout.

Five years have passed. Herren has made a success of his venture, but times are better now and he is hankering for a different life. Into his place walk Guido and Amalia Negri. Guido, a dapper Italian-American, has impeccable restaurant credentials, as former chef for President Wilson on the USS *George Washington* and as superintendent of the Atlanta Biltmore dining room. Now he wants a place of his own. He makes Herren an offer he can't refuse. Fadeout.

Three years have passed, and the Negris have expanded and improved the restaurant, adding among other things airconditioning, the wave of the future. Unexpectedly, Guido dies and, in the middle of a war, Amalia must carry on alone, feeding countless soldiers and civilians on rationing. Fadeout.

The war over, son Ed returns to help out with the restaurant. He remodels several times, adding in 1958 Atlanta's first lobster tank, which sits in the front window and is an instant tourist attraction. Atlanta grows, and so does Herren's, which has by now become an institution among Atlanta businessmen. In 1984 Ed Negri realizes a dream; he opens an adjoining companion restaurant, naming it Guido's after his father.

Last scene: Ed Negri, now in his sixties, takes a moment to sit down in Guido's with some reminiscent customers. "Why shouldn't we be good?" he grins. "We've had the same good cooks for thirty years." He points out the pictures on the wall, photos of Atlanta in the thirties and forties. Herren's was there then, when Atlanta's skyline was much shorter than it is now.

Herren's was feeding Atlanta when Atlantans came to work on the trolley, and it's still feeding them today.

Herren's and Guido's are at 84 Luckie Street, NW in Atlanta. Both open Monday through Friday at 11:00 a.m.; Herren's closes at 2:30 p.m., and Guido's is open all afternoon, serving the lunch menu all day until 8:00 p.m. For information and reservations call (404) 525-1712.

HERREN'S SHRIMP DE JONGHE

de Jonghe Butter:
1 clove garlic, finely chopped
2 sticks butter, softened
½ teaspoon Worcestershire sauce
½ lemon rind, grated
¼ orange rind, grated
salt and freshly ground pepper to taste

In a wooden bowl crush the garlic with a wooden spoon. Add the butter and blend, then add the other ingredients. Wrap butter tightly and refrigerate for at least a day before using. Leftover butter may be frozen in pats for later use.

Sauce:
4 tablespoons butter
4 tablespoons flour
2 cups chicken broth
salt to taste
¼ teaspoon white pepper
¼ teaspoon cayenne pepper
½ cup heavy cream
1 teaspoon lemon juice
1 teaspoon Worcestershire sauce
1 teaspoon paprika
¼ cup dry sherry

To make the sauce, melt the butter, remove it from heat and stir in the flour, cooking and stirring for 1 minute. Do not brown. Add the chicken stock and cook and stir until the sauce is thickened. Add salt and pepper. Beat in the cream, a tablespoon at a time, until the sauce is the desired thickness. Do not boil. Add other sauce ingredients and blend well.

1½ to 2 pounds jumbo shrimp
5 cups cooked brown rice

Prepare the rice and steam, peel and devein the shrimp. Place the cooked rice in 5 or 6 individual ramekins or in a casserole. Top with the sauce and the cooked shrimp. Lay about 20 pats of the de Jonghe Butter around on top of the shrimp. Bake at 450 degrees until bubbly. Serves 5 or 6.

HERREN'S SWEET ROLLS

1 cup milk	¼ cup warm water
4 tablespoons butter	4 cups flour, sifted
¼ cup sugar	2 cups sugar
1¼ teaspoons salt	4 teaspoons cinnamon
2 packages yeast	

Let the milk come to a boil in a heavy saucepan. Add butter, sugar and salt. Cool. Soften the yeast in the warm water and stir into the first mixture. Add flour, about half at a time, and beat well. Turn out on a floured board, allow dough to sit for 15 minutes, then knead until smooth. Place the dough in a buttered bowl, cover with a cloth and let rise until double in size.

Roll out on a floured board until dough is about ¼-inch thick, and cut it into roughly 8-inch squares. Work with one square at a time. Brush with melted butter. Mix the cinnamon and sugar and sprinkle some of it over the entire surface. Starting at one side of the square, roll dough up into a tube. Continue rolling the tube back and forth until it is 12 to 16 inches long. Roll all the squares and cut the tubes into wheels that are approximately ½-inch wide; place them flat in aluminum pans that have been brushed with melted butter and sprinkled generously with the cinnamon-sugar mixture. Place rolls in the pans so that they touch, but don't overpack. Brush the tops with butter and sprinkle cinnamon-sugar mixture generously over the entire surface. Let rolls stand at room temperature for an hour before baking. The rolls can then be baked at 350 degrees for 18 to 20 minutes. (Or cover with aluminum foil and refrigerate for later use. Allow 30 minutes to bring dough back to room temperature before baking.) Yields 60 to 80 rolls.

LE PAPILLON RESTAURANT IN INMAN PARK
Atlanta

LE PAPILLON RESTAURANT IN INMAN PARK

Inman Park in the 1890s was an Atlanta suburb, street after street of ten-room Victorian cottages and grander, turreted places in which many Atlanta notables lived. Over time the notables moved away, the neighborhood slowly declined, and by the 1950s it was mainly a series of one-room, weekly rental houses. The historic preservationists got in just ahead of the wrecking ball and began proving once again that years of gut-wrenching hard work and millions of dollars can restore a neighborhood to something of its former grandeur. Le Papillon is a piece of that work.

The contractor who constructed many of the homes in Inman Park built Le Papillon for himself and lived in it for thirty years, after which a Mr. Samples, the trolley car operator, and his family were in residence for a while. Then the place did a stint as a sign shop and grocery store before being acquired in 1978 by George Wilson, who started the restaurant.

Le Papillon is comprised of four rooms with fireplaces, oak wainscotting and lace curtains. If you're looking for glitz, don't go there. It's a place filled with pottery rather than fine china, understated to the point of being unfinished. Its owner devotes his time to raising the herbs with which he seasons the food, shopping for the freshest vegetables and cooking. His priorities are obvious as soon as you sample the food, which is excellent.

It's a place to go on an early spring evening when you feel careless and, if you're old enough, nostalgic for the '60s. Then you might wander over to Le Papillon for a bowl of Oysters Florentine soup, and Poached Fish with Vouvray and Bittersweet Chocolate Cake. Or in the fall when the leaves are turning yellow and you feel melancholy, you can console yourself with a loaf of homemade bread, Sautéed Carrots and Snow Peas and Breast of Chicken with Eggplant Stuffing. You also can spend a Victorian Christmas there and find, one way or another, whatever you need to feed your soul. It's not named the butterfly for nothing.

Le Papillon is located at 785 Edgewood Avenue Northeast in Inman Park in Atlanta. It is open every day for dinner from 6:30 p.m. until 10:00 p.m. For reservations call (404) 688-2172.

LE PAPILLON'S BREAST OF CHICKEN WITH EGGPLANT STUFFING

8 boneless, skinless, whole chicken breasts
½ cup olive oil
Marinade (recipe follows)
Eggplant Stuffing (recipe follows)
Tarragon Sauce (recipe follows)

Arrange the chicken breasts in a glass or stainless steel dish, and pour the marinade over the chicken. Refrigerate the chicken breasts overnight in the marinade. The next day dry the chicken and sauté in olive oil until barely firm and lightly brown. Do not overcook. Put the chicken on a serving plate and sauté the Eggplant Stuffing briefly to reheat. Divide it among the chicken breasts, placing about ¼ cup between two halves, sandwich-style, for each serving. Pour brown Tarragon Sauce on top of chicken and serve. Serves 8.

Marinade:
1 teaspoon rosemary sprigs
¼ cup olive oil
juice of 1 whole lemon
salt and pepper to taste
1 clove garlic
¼ cup soy sauce

Mix all the ingredients together in a blender or food processor.

Eggplant Stuffing:
1 eggplant
⅓ to ½ cup olive oil
1 medium onion, minced
1 small, red bell pepper, chopped
1 clove garlic, finely minced
salt and pepper to taste

Peel the eggplant and cut it into ¼-inch cubes; salt heavily and drain in a colander for 30 minutes. Dry the cubes on a towel and sauté, one layer at a time, in olive oil until lightly browned on all sides. Drain on paper towels. Sauté the minced onions until translucent and add the bell peppers, sautéing until soft. Return the eggplant to the pan with the onions and peppers, adding the garlic, salt and pepper. Continue to sauté until mushy and well combined.

Tarragon Sauce:

2 tablespoons cornstarch
½ cup unsalted chicken stock or water
1 11-ounce can beef bouillon
¼ cup port wine
dash of pepper
pinch of tarragon

Mix the cornstarch with the chicken stock or water and add it to the beef bouillon, to make two cups of liquid. Heat, adding port wine, pepper and tarragon to taste, stirring constantly until thickened. Reduce, adding port wine as necessary to enrich the sauce.

ATKIN'S PARK RESTAURANT
Atlanta

ATKINS PARK RESTAURANT

In 1925 the Atlanta suburb of Virginia Highlands was an exceedingly nice place to live—a bit far out, to be sure, but the streetcar ran right downtown, and the houses were absolutely the latest style. At Atkins Park there was even a small commercial district with shops and a little delicatessen. On a nice day you could take a stroll right down to the market or, if you preferred, order something delivered. The atmosphere was refined—peaceful suburbia with style.

In 1987 Virginia Highlands is still an exceedingly nice place to live—a tad close in, maybe, but the houses are really adorable, and it's just minutes from everywhere. The kids can practically walk to school. Plus it has all the perks—bookstores, shops and a variety of restaurants that you can wander into for a bite on your way home from work or play.

Take Atkins Park Restaurant, for instance. The building used to be a deli in the 1920s, then became a tavern and has been one ever since, although it currently houses a first-class restaurant too. You enter the restaurant through the bar, still adorned with tin ceiling, tile floor and an enormous, comfortable bar. Booths line one wall, and you can eat there if you like. For dinner, though, you might prefer the dining room, with soft cream and green colors as well as tablecloths and flowers to abet a relaxed meal.

The food at Atkins Park is something you'll want to take time to savor. For lunch your choices include burgers, soups, sandwiches and enormous salads. Or try a Pasta Plate—fettucini or vermicelli with tempting toppings like primavera vegetables, poached oysters or baby shrimp. For dinner you might start with Salmon and Boursin Crêpes or my favorite, Artichoke Hearts Savannah, proceeding in a leisurely manner to Pepper Steak, Gnocchi, Trout, or any of several chicken dishes. For dessert there is always Chocolate Grand Marnier Mousse. While sipping your coffee, note the two stained-glass phoenixes, the restaurant logo, and the pictures of old Atlanta which adorn the walls. There may be more pleasant ways to absorb a history lesson, but I can't think of even one offhand.

Atkins Park Restaurant is located at 794 North Highland Avenue in Atlanta. It is open for lunch from 11:00 a.m. to 3:00 p.m. Monday through Friday, and for brunch on Saturday and Sunday. Dinner is served from 5:30 p.m. to 11:00 p.m. Sunday through Thursday, and from 5:30 p.m. to midnight on Friday and Saturday. In the bar, food can be ordered from the lunch menu any time. For reservations call (404) 876-7249.

ATKINS PARK RESTAURANT'S CHICKEN MEDITERRANEAN

6 deboned chicken breasts
salt and pepper to taste
dash of marjoram
12 ounces of fresh spinach
1 8-ounce jar feta cheese
½ cup white wine
½ stick butter

Remove skin from chicken and lightly flatten the chicken breasts with your hand; season them with salt, pepper and marjoram. Wilt the spinach by sautéing it in butter or by blanching it in boiling water for a minute. Drain the spinach thoroughly and spread leaves on the chicken. Place a "finger" of feta cheeese on top of each piece of chicken, then roll the chicken breasts, placing them in a casserole dish with the seams down. Add wine and a pat of butter for each breast and bake at 350 degrees for 25 minutes. If enough wine and butter are used, they make a perfect accompanying sauce. Serves 6.

ATKINS PARK RESTAURANT'S ARTICHOKE HEARTS SAVANNAH

2 14-ounce cans artichoke hearts (or 1 can artichoke bottoms)
1 cup sherry
6 ounces crabmeat
8 ounces cream cheese, softened
2 tablespoons fresh dill, chopped
3 tablespoons Parmesan cheese
salt and pepper to taste
lemon juice from ¼ lemon

Marinate the artichoke hearts or bottoms in sherry by bringing them to a boil and allowing them to cool. Reserve the sherry. Remove the shell bits and cartilage from the crabmeat. Mix together the crab, cream cheese, dill, Parmesan cheese, salt, pepper and lemon juice. If a looser consistency is desired for the filling, add a little of the sherry to the mix. Stuff the artichokes with a generous amount of the filling and sprinkle with more Parmesan cheese. Bake in a casserole at 375 degrees until golden brown on top, about 12 minutes. (If a sauce is desired, thicken the sherry with a tablespoon of cornstarch dissolved in water and stirred, over heat, into the sherry.) Serves 4.

THE ABBEY
Atlanta

THE ABBEY

The Abbey caters to those of us who saw *Becket* three times and cherish a fondness for a medieval atmosphere. Here you dine in a converted church sanctuary, under a fifty-foot vaulted ceiling. Easing into your leather-covered bishop's chair, you take in the gleaming table setting, the fresh flowers on your table. Shadows dance on the walls in the flickering light, and you wish you had worn your velvet. Then a monkish waiter brings you a menu, and you get down to the business at hand, selecting a meal from an incredible array of culinary jewels.

The menu is full of delicious-sounding food that could be featured in gourmet magazines—and, in fact, sometimes is. There is Galantine of Duckling with Lingonberries, Spinach and Fois Gras Salad with Hot Bacon Dressing and Baked Oysters with Scallops and Bay Shrimp. And those are just the appetizers. The entrées include most anything you'd want from a continental menu: fish, fowl, beef, veal, lamb or venison. And be sure to save room for a Praline Tulip or some Benedictine-laced coffee. You may waddle home feeling like Charles Laughton playing Henry VIII, but never mind. Unlike Henry, you won't have to get up the next morning and ride to hounds.

The Abbey has been a renowned Atlanta restaurant for twenty years, earning international food and wine awards all along the way. Formerly a Methodist-Episcopal church, the 1915 structure reflects the passion for Gothic Revival architecture which dominated the end of the Victorian period. During the day the massive arched windows let in an abundance of refracted light. And don't get so caught up in your Lobster Thermidor that you fail to notice the stained glass, which is gorgeous, especially the ceiling in the Abbot's Cup Lounge.

The early church fathers appreciated how worshippers' senses became more alert and finely tuned in the rich and lofty air of a cathedral. The Abbey works on the same principle. Whatever your experience there, it's certain to be unlike any other church supper you've ever had.

The Abbey is located at 163 Ponce de Leon Avenue in Atlanta. The lounge opens every day at 5:00 p.m. for cocktails. The restaurant opens at 6:00 p.m. daily; the last seating is at 10:45 p.m. Banquet facilities are available for business luncheons, receptions and other special events. Reservations are recommended; call (404) 876-8532.

THE ABBEY'S FRENCH BRIE SOUP

¼ cup butter
2 cups diced onions
¼ teaspoon diced garlic
1 cup sliced mushrooms
1 cup dry white wine
¼ cup flour
3½ cups chicken stock or broth
1 bay leaf
pinch freshly chopped thyme
1¼ pints heavy whipping cream
10 ounces Brie cheese, cut into slices
salt and pepper to taste
2 ounces sherry
12 toasted croutons

Melt the butter in a saucepan and sauté the onions, garlic and mushrooms. Add the wine and reduce until almost dry. Add flour and work the mixture into a paste over low heat. Add the chicken stock and the bay leaf, bring to a boil, and simmer until a soup consistency is achieved. Add the thyme and whipping cream. Strain the soup and replace on heat. Slowly, using a whisk, blend in 6 ounces of the Brie, whipping until smooth. Add salt, pepper and sherry to taste. Pour into bowls, top with croutons, and lay the remaining slices of Brie on the croutons. Brown lightly under a broiler and serve. Serves 6.

THE ABBEY'S PRALINE TULIPS

Pralines:
1⅓ cups light brown sugar
1 cup light Karo syrup
2 sticks unsalted butter
2 cups chopped pecans and/or almonds
2 cups flour

Bring the sugar, Karo syrup and butter to a boil over medium heat. Remove from heat; add chopped pecans or almonds and flour to the syrup and mix well. Preheat the oven to 325 degrees and prepare sheet pans by covering with parchment and spraying the paper with nonstick cooking spray. Spoon the mixture onto the paper, making rounds of approximately 6 inches in diameter. Bake for 10 to 15 minutes until the pralines can be lifted from the parchment without breaking. When bubbles subside, carefully place the pralines onto inverted soup cups. They will droop and form a cup. Let them stand until hard. Store pralines in plastic containers between layers of parchment paper. Yields approximately 15 pralines, depending on their size.

Filling:
2 pints sliced strawberries **15 pecan halves for garnish**
½ gallon vanilla ice cream

Just prior to serving, fill with sliced strawberries, top with vanilla ice cream and garnish with one slice of strawberry and one pecan half.

THE ABBEY'S APRICOT SOUP

2 pounds dried apricots **4 tablespoons lemon juice**
¾ cup sauterne or Barsac **1 cup sugar**
6 cups whipping cream **pinch of salt**
1 cup sour cream **orange peel and mint**
1 teaspoon cinnamon **leaves for garnish**
¼ teaspoon nutmeg

Soak the apricots overnight in the white wine and cream; drain and reserve the liquid. Purée the apricots and add the puréed fruit to the cream and wine blend. Add the remaining ingredients, reserving ¼ cup of the sour cream for garnish. Pass all of this mixture through cheesecloth to the serving container, discarding the pulp after it has been squeezed dry. Chill and top with a spoonful of sour cream garnished with orange peel and mint leaves. Serves 6.

HARRY BISSETT'S NEW ORLEANS CAFE & OYSTER BAR
Athens

HARRY BISSETT'S NEW ORLEANS CAFE AND OYSTER BAR

Athens, Georgia, like its Mediterranean namesake, is awash in historic buildings. Both cities went in for classical columns in a big way, and both are seats of learning and scholarship. Never mind if the antiquities are a tad more antique in Athens, Greece; all there is outside the Parthenon is a lemonade stand. Outside the gates of the University of Georgia is Harry Bissett's New Orleans Cafe and Oyster Bar.

There you can find a fried-oyster sandwich that will rival any you have eaten anywhere, a perfect Cajun Martini and a Seafood Jambalaya that will warm you all the way down, in approved south-Louisiana style. And where else can you find Maque Choux? Pronounced mock shoe, both the name and recipe for this delicious dish are "cajunizations" of a traditional corn and tomato stew popular with the Indians inhabiting South Louisiana before the Acadian migrations.

Harry Bissett's has something else too—the style of a New Orleans restaurant. New Orleans knows something about hanging out that the rest of the world has yet to master, but Harry Bissett's comes close to capturing the secret, possibly because it is near a college known for its laid-back style. It has practically the only bar in Georgia where small children can belly up and swill a cola and a few fries with their daddies without getting stared at.

Beyond the bar are more tables, situated upstairs and down in a courtyard covered with a skylight. For more formal dining there is a yellow and green room upstairs which used to be the site of board meetings back when Harry Bissett's was the University Bank of Athens. It has been meticulously and expensively restored, even to the tin ceiling, which was replaced with an authentic duplicate. Sit by a window and take a moment to look out at the Bradford pear trees and consider: only in this place have ancient Greece, old New Orleans and a small-town southern bank mingled their flavors in a gumbo so delightful.

Harry Bissett's New Orleans Cafe and Oyster Bar is located at 279 East Broad Street in Athens. Lunch is served Monday through Friday from 11:30 a.m. until 3:00 p.m.; on Saturday there is a New Orleans-style brunch. Dinner is served from 5:30 p.m. until 10:00 p.m. Monday through Thursday, and from 5:30 p.m. until 11:00 p.m. on Friday and Saturday. For additional information call (404) 353-7065.

HARRY BISSETT'S MAQUE CHOUX

8 ears of cleaned corn
½ cup coarsely chopped onions
½ cup chopped bell peppers
1 cup peeled and chopped tomatoes (or 1 cup canned stewed tomatoes)
1 teaspoon sugar
1 teaspoon black pepper
¼ teaspoon white pepper
¼ teaspoon cayenne pepper
¼ teaspoon Tabasco sauce
1 teaspoon salt
½ teaspoon thyme
½ teaspoon basil
2 whole bay leaves
½ cup chopped scallions
¼ cup chopped parsley
½ cup vegetable oil

With a sharp knife, cut the corn kernels in half lengthwise, then cut them off the cobs. Scrape the cobs with the back of the knife to remove the pulp and milk of the corn. Mix all ingredients except the oil. In a large iron skillet, heat the oil and add the corn mixture. Be careful, as popping will occur. Lower the heat and simmer, covered, for 45 minutes, stirring occasionally. Serves 4 to 6.

HARRY BISSETT'S CHICKEN PONTALBA

Potato Mixture:
1½ sticks butter
5 potatoes, peeled and diced
½ bunch green onions, chopped
1 tablespoon minced garlic
1 pound cubed ham
1½ cups sliced mushrooms
2 tablespoons chopped parsley
½ teaspoon salt
1 teaspoon black pepper
½ teaspoon cayenne pepper
½ teaspoon basil
1 cup white wine

In a large skillet, melt the butter and sauté the potatoes, onions and garlic on low heat for about 15 minutes, until potatoes are browned. Add other ingredients and sauté another 10 minutes. Remove with a slotted spoon and keep warm while preparing the sauce and chicken. Reserve the butter-wine liquid left in the skillet.

Béarnaise Sauce:
6 egg yolks	½ teaspoon white vinegar
2 sticks softened butter	¼ cup shallots, finely chopped
¼ teaspoon salt	
⅛ teaspoon cayenne pepper	2 tablespoons tarragon
½ tablespoon fresh lemon juice	1 tablespoon butter
¾ cup Burgundy wine	

In a double boiler, whisk egg yolks about 2 minutes over low heat. Slowly add softened butter, whisking constantly until sauce thickens. Continue whisking as you remove it from heat. Add salt, pepper and lemon juice. This is a Hollandaise Sauce.

Put the Burgundy, vinegar, shallots, tarragon and 1 tablespoon of butter in a small saucepan and reduce them by simmering until all the liquid has evaporated. Add this mixture to the Hollandaise. Keep sauce at room temperature while preparing the chicken.

Chicken:
1 teaspoon salt	4 chicken breasts, deboned and halved
¼ teaspoon black pepper	
¼ teaspoon cayenne pepper	1 cup vegetable oil
1 cup flour	

Combine the seasonings and flour, and dredge the chicken pieces in this seasoned flour. Add oil to the reserved butter in the skillet in which the potatoes were fried, and heat until the butter sizzles. Fry the chicken, turning often, until golden brown (about 10 minutes).

Serve in casserole or au gratin dishes with the potatoes on bottom, then a layer of chicken, and lots of Béarnaise Sauce on top. Serves 4.

FOX HOLLOW
Madison

FOX HOLLOW

On a cold night in November, your first stop at Fox Hollow might be the cozy bar that sits at the back of the house. The Rasches have named it the Right Whale, in honor of the whale which feeds in waters off the coast of Georgia. If, like the whale, you hail from around New England and get lonely occasionally for a wood stove and a Vermont-like sort of place to have a beer, you'll feel right at home. Not that it's all dolled up with things to provide "atmosphere." It's just comfortable.

After warming your toes, you can adjourn for a dinner selected from a simple and tempting menu that features seafood, chicken, quail, an assortment of vegetables and homemade breads. I particularly like the Country Dinner, which includes an unusual and delicious vegetable dish, Carrots and Rutabagas Baked with Shallots. An appetizer, salad, entrée, dessert and glass of wine will set you back about fifteen dollars.

Fox Hollow began life as an overseer's house, part of an antebellum plantation. The "big" house fell down years ago, having stood empty for a long time. The overseer's house fared better, doing a stint as a dairy before its conversion ten years ago into a restaurant. Over the years it has been modified and added onto, and today it is a large, Piedmont-plain farmhouse, with plenty of fireplaces and a wraparound porch that the Rasches have enclosed for dining. They have kept the décor plain and unpretentious, adding gray and mustard paint, lace curtains and, curiously, an old carousel horse.

Though Fox Hollow stands a mere two or three miles from Madison and a bare half-mile south of I-20, when you visit you'll feel like you're in the deep country. The restaurant sits beside a big field, and behind and beyond it the woods edge up over the hill. The old family cemetery in the front yard attests that a family named Tucker once owned it all, way before the Civil War. Madison and environs were on the stagecoach route from Charleston to New Orleans, and the area supported a thriving community long before Atlanta became a major city. Fox Hollow and its plantation were a part of that culture and time. Thanks to the influence of Senator Hill, who knew General Sherman's family (and who used his influence to persuade Sherman to spare his town), and to the industry of the local historical society, most of the antebellum homes in Madison are still standing and still being lived in, for us tourists to gawk at on our way to dine at Fox Hollow. Don't miss a look. It may be your last chance to see nineteenth-century Georgia intact.

Fox Hollow is located at 2330 Eatonton Road in Madison (on Highway 441, one-half mile south of I-20). It is open for dinner Tuesday through Saturday at 6:00 p.m., and there is a buffet luncheon each Sunday from 11:30 a.m. until 2:00 p.m. Fox Hollow is closed during January. For reservations call (404) 342-4400.

FOX HOLLOW'S CAJUN SALAD

Salad:
assorted salad greens (a mix of lettuce, romaine, turnips, spinach)
4 cooked artichoke hearts (fresh, frozen or canned)
8 to 12 black olives

In a salad bowl, toss the greens, artichoke hearts and black olives with the dressing. Serves 4.

Dressing:
1 to 2 cloves garlic
½ teaspoon salt
1 or 2 artichoke hearts
3 tablespoons olive oil
1 tablespoon lemon juice
dash of Louisiana Hot Sauce (optional)
dash of Worcestershire sauce (optional)

In a food processor or blender, crush and mash the garlic and add the salt and one large or two small artichoke hearts. Blend until puréed. Add the olive oil and lemon juice, as well as the hot sauce and Worcestershire sauce if desired. Blend.

FOX HOLLOW'S CARROTS AND RUTABAGAS BAKED WITH SHALLOTS

1 rutabaga or large turnip (¾ pound)
4 carrots (¾ pound)
4 shallots
1½ cups chicken stock
4 tablespoons butter
3 tablespoons sugar
⅛ teaspoon nutmeg
½ cup heavy cream
3 eggs
salt and pepper to taste

Trim carrots and rutabaga into ½-inch chunks. Combine carrots, rutabagas, shallots, chicken stock, butter, sugar and nutmeg; cook until tender. Transfer only the vegetables to a food processor, and boil the remaining liquid to reduce it. Add the reduced liquid (about ¼ cup) to the vegetables and purée smooth. Add the cream and process again. When the mixture has cooled, whisk in the eggs and season to taste. Pour into a greased casserole and bake at 350 degrees for 50 to 60 minutes. Serves 4.

FOX HOLLOW'S SWEET AND PUNGENT PORK

1½ pounds lean pork, cut into ½-inch cubes
¼ cup oil
2 green peppers, sliced
2½ cups sliced apples
1 cup chicken stock
3 tablespoons cornstarch
2 to 3 tablespoons soy sauce
½ cup vinegar
½ cup sugar
½ teaspoon salt
¼ teaspoon pepper

Place cubed pork and oil in a skillet. Brown the pork on all sides over medium heat. Add the green peppers, apples and a third of the chicken stock. Simmer for 20 minutes, covered. In a small bowl blend the remaining stock, cornstarch, soy sauce, vinegar, sugar, salt and pepper. Add the mixture slowly to the simmering pork mix. Cook, stirring, until the sauce thickens. Serve over rice, if desired. Serves 4 to 6.

THE DEPOT AT COVINGTON
Covington

THE DEPOT AT COVINGTON

Thoreau hated trains. He said they were ugly, noisy and smelly, and they frightened the animals. He may have been right, but other citizens welcomed trains anyway because they were also fast and reliable. And exciting. By the middle of the nineteenth century a couple could hop a train to spend a few days in a faraway place and be back again in practically no time at all. A farmer could load his crops on a train and have them to market in a day, instead of the week or two it would have taken by wagon. A young teacher stuck in the wilds of west Georgia could go home to visit her folks for Christmas. The possibilities for sociability as well as commerce were infinitely increased.

The railroad came to Covington in 1845. The first depot was wooden, replaced in 1880 by a fine brick one which still stands, once again a gathering place for people on the move. Only now it's a restaurant. The lead glass framing the front door gives you a clue that the Depot wasn't restored in a low-budget, paint-and-a-prayer fashion. The impression is confirmed inside. The little entranceway has a "terminal" where you check in and out, complete with pictures of old Covington. Ahead is the bar, formerly the ticket counter, and small cocktail booths and tables where you can sit and relax a while. To the right, the dining room spreads out to a grill at the far end. It's all as spiffy and comfortable as it can be, in soothing maroon and brown colors.

The food is soothing too. For lunch you can get things like a Chef Salad, Philadelphia Steak Sandwich or Deep-fried Shrimp for five or six dollars. The dinner menu changes weekly, typically offering entrées like Blackened Red Snapper, Cajun Seafood Platter and Veal a la Michelle. I tried the Sole Oscar and the Chicken Fettucini, and both were superb.

You can have such a nice, relaxed meal at the Depot that you forget you're in a train station, but try and remember as you leave to go out to look at the train cars rowed up behind the restaurant to house the offices and private dining rooms. You might even go home whistling "Casey Jones" and dig out your old Lionel train set.

The Depot at Covington is located at 4122 North Emory Street in Covington. It is open for lunch Monday through Friday from 11:30 a.m. until 2:30 p.m., and for dinner Monday through Saturday evenings from 5:30 until 10:00. Sunday, the Depot is open for lunch only, from 11:30 a.m. until 2:00 p.m. For reservations call (404) 787-6400.

THE DEPOT'S CHICKEN FETTUCINI

1 cup clarified butter
4 fresh cloves garlic, chopped
4 cups clam juice
2 teaspoons chopped parsley
salt to taste
1 teaspoon pepper
1 teaspoon oregano
4 cups minced clams
12 ounces fettucini noodles
1½ pounds chicken breasts, skinned and boned
salt and pepper to taste
½ clarified butter
1¼ cups heavy cream

Melt the butter in a skillet and sauté the garlic until lightly browned. Gradually add the clam juice and stir in the parsley, salt, pepper and oregano. Add the clams and cook until clams are heated through. Set sauce aside.

Begin cooking the noodles according to package directions. While the fettucini is cooking, slice the chicken into strips, salt and pepper them and sauté in clarified butter until light golden and just done. Over low heat, stir in the clam sauce and cream. Do not boil. When the noodles are done, drain, rinse them with hot water, and drain them again. Then toss the noodles with the chicken-clam mixture over low heat, just to warm the noodles, and serve. Serves 2 to 4.

THE DEPOT'S SOLE OSCAR

1 pound asparagus (18 spears)
6 6-ounce sole fillets
salt and pepper to taste
flour for coating fish
3 eggs, slightly beaten
4 tablespoons clarified butter
9 ounces crabmeat, snow or lump
1½ cups Hollandaise Sauce (see Index)

Cook the asparagus in water until just tender; do not overcook. Drain and set spears aside. Season the sole fillets with salt and pepper and dip them in flour to coat lightly, then into slightly beaten egg to cover completely. Place some of the clarified butter in a medium-hot pan and sauté the sole on each side until light golden brown and just done (40 seconds on each side). Remove pan from heat. In another pan, sauté the crabmeat in a little of the clarified butter just to heat through. Sauté the asparagus in a third pan, in the last of the clarified butter. Place three asparagus spears on each portion of sole and top with crabmeat. Cover with Hollandaise Sauce. Serves 6.

THE VERANDA
Senoia

THE VERANDA

The Veranda is the sort of place you go when you want to give someone a little treat. Your mom might be visiting for a few days, or maybe your son had a good report card, or you wake up on a sunny Saturday and decide you want a drive through the country. So you call Jan and Bobby Boal and say, "May we come for lunch?" And they say, "Yes, what would you like to eat?" And you say, "Oh, anything, with some of those little bitty rolls."

When you get there, you enter a large, white, country-Victorian house—and you are immediately charmed. Built in 1907 as a hotel, the Veranda is primarily a bed-and-breakfast establishment now. It looks remarkably like Great-aunt Louise's house, or Great-uncle John's, with the same big rockers on the porch and a screen door that slams. The parlors and sitting rooms are full of bric-a-brac to look at and admire. Your daughter is enchanted with some paperweights. Your mother says, "I remember we used to have an old Victrola just like this when I was a child." Your son runs straight down the hall to the umbrella stand and starts digging for the sword cane. Mr. Boal helps him. He also shows him a new monkey puzzle they've acquired. Then lunch is ready.

The dining room is plain, decorated in season with jars of wildflowers. The tablecloths are homemade. "I don't want anybody to feel like we're pretentious," says Mrs. Boal. Mr. Boal brings homemade crackers and iced tea and then, in unhurried succession, a series of little delights—a cold salad made with five or six different fresh fruits, Cold Peach Soup, a basket of the special Angel Rolls, a pot of Thyme Jelly and some butter, a casserole called Chicken and Ham Veranda. Some more rolls. Your children, who hate squash at home, say, "Mom, what are these delicious yellow circles?" For dessert the children choose Brownies and Ice Cream and get a concoction that looks like the Eiffel Tower, which they demolish with squeals of delight. The other adults get Peach Shortcake, matchstick-size slivers of fresh peaches atop homemade pound cake, slathered with cream. You order Scuppernong Pie, wondering if you have made a mistake. You haven't.

After lunch, if they aren't too busy, the Boals might give you a tour of the bedrooms or demonstrate some of the kaleidoscopes in the gift shop. They collect handmade games and toys for sale to museum shops, so they have a lot of that kind of thing lying around. Or you might prefer just to sit on the veranda and rock for a while. You feel really good. You think, "It's so nice here. When can I come again? Who'll I bring next time? Who do I know who needs this kind of magic?" And pretty soon you think of someone, and you smile. Because, after all, you'll get to come too.

The Veranda is located at 252 Seavy Street in Senoia. It is open for brunch, lunch and dinner; however there are no specific set hours. Meals are served by reservation only. The Veranda can accommodate a diabetic or other restricted diet. For reservations (required) call (404) 599-3905.

THE VERANDA'S
SWEET GEORGIA BROWN BREAD

1 stick butter
1 cup graham cracker crumbs
¾ cup cornmeal
½ cup whole wheat flour
½ cup sifted all-purpose flour
¼ cup wheat germ
2 teaspoons soda
1½ teaspoons baking powder
¾ teaspoon salt
½ teaspoon cinnamon
½ teaspoon freshly grated nutmeg
¾ cup molasses
2 cups buttermilk
1 cup raisins and/or chopped dates

Melt the stick of butter in the top of a steamer, over boiling water. In a separate bowl mix together all the dry ingredients. Mix the buttermilk and molasses together, and stir them into the dry ingredients, beating well with a spoon. Pour mixture into the butter in the top of the steamer, and sprinkle the raisins and dates over the batter. Cover with a lid and steam for three hours. Serve hot with butter or softened cream cheese. Yields 1 loaf.

THE VERANDA'S SQUASH

2 or 3 yellow squash
2 or more tablespoons butter
dash of coarsely ground pepper
pinch of basil
pinch of oregano
dash of Italian herb seasoning
1 tablespoon green onion tops, chopped

Slice the neck of the squash in thin rounds, and cut the fat part into matchstick-size pieces (or use only the necks for this recipe, reserving the larger part for a casserole). Sauté the squash in butter, sprinkling it with pepper, basil, oregano and herb seasoning. Sauté just until tender, only a minute or two. Just before serving, drop in the onion tops and stir. To vary, use zucchini as well as yellow squash, or add a few pimientos. Serves 4.

SOMETHING SPECIAL
Newnan

SOMETHING SPECIAL In spite of the vagaries of war and time, Georgia still has its share of antebellum mansions. While researching historic restaurants in Georgia I began to wonder, after a while, if General Sherman was not really a figment of the Confederate imagination. There are, after all, extravagant dinners to be had in Atlanta mansions and coastal plantations, sweet little luncheons in sweet little drawing rooms and cottages, memorable brunches beneath an assortment of columns and porticos. But at least one antebellum home in Georgia houses an authentic tea room, a vanishing species that now exists mainly in rural England and the American South, where it serves a valuable and valid service.

Something Special in Newnan is a true tea room. Owned and operated by Martha Sue McCain and her mother Virginia Davis, the restaurant consists of four lovely rooms on the ground floor of an 1850s southern home. The owners live upstairs. The Cardinal and Dogwood rooms still have the huge stained-glass windows, sparkling chandeliers and marble fireplaces placed there by the original owners, the Banks-St. John family, more than a century ago. Even so, the place is homey, not fancy. I think Mrs. St. John would have approved. She certainly would have approved of the food. "After all," says McCain, "we only fix things that we like, because we have to eat what's left over for supper."

Five days a week they serve forty or fifty people lunch— typically quiches, soups, salads, vegetables, a basket of bread and dessert—for about four dollars per person. More hearty than a traditional quiche, the Sausage-Cheddar Quiche reminded me of a Mexican-style meat pie. On a cold day try the Hot Curried Fruit and Chicken Hawaiian. And when you need something cooler, the Garden Salad and homemade cold soups offer a soothing reprieve from the heat. Something Special also sells a lot of cakes and baked goods, thus allowing the citizens of Newnan considerable leeway in the matter of entertaining.

"I like for people to feel at home," says McCain. To that end, she has decorated with her own needlepoint and collections of china plates and figurines. She also likes to throw parties, like her annual Grandmother-Granddaughter Tea and special holiday feasts. A local bridge club meets there weekly, in the Magnolia Room. In general, though, the raison d'être of the tea room is to feed people quickly and inexpensively and allow them to chat, a pleasant respite in a bustling world.

Something Special is located at 83 Greenville Street in Newnan. It is open for lunch from 11:00 a.m. to 2:00 p.m. every day but Wednesday and Sunday. Evenings are set aside for special parties. Reservations are recommended for large groups. Call (404) 253-5513.

SOMETHING SPECIAL'S SAUSAGE-CHEDDAR QUICHE

Cornmeal Pastry:
¾ cup self-rising cornmeal
¾ cup self-rising flour
⅓ cup shortening
2 to 4 tablespoons ice water

Combine the cornmeal and flour. Cut or rub in shortening until the mixture is crumbly. Add enough water so that the dough begins to stick together. Turn the dough out onto a sheet of waxed paper and press it together. Cover with a second sheet of waxed paper and roll the dough out to fit a 9-inch or 10-inch pie pan. Peel the paper off one side and flip the dough into the pan, peeling the second sheet off after you've gotten the crust placed correctly. Trim off excess. Prick the bottom of the crust several times with a fork and bake it for about 8 minutes in a preheated 425-degree oven.

Sausage-Cheddar Filling:
1 pound hot sausage
1 4-ounce can sliced mushrooms (or ½ cup sliced fresh mushrooms)
½ cup chopped onions
¼ cup chopped green peppers
1 teaspoon minced parsley
½ teaspoon whole basil leaves
dash of granulated garlic
1½ cups shredded cheese
1 cup milk
2 eggs
dash of paprika

Crumble the sausage into a frying pan and cook until brown; drain. Add the mushrooms, onions, green peppers, parsley, basil, garlic and salt, mixing well. Spoon sausage mixture into the prepared pastry shell and sprinkle with the cheese. In a bowl combine the milk and eggs, beating just until foamy. Pour evenly over the cheese. Sprinkle with paprika and bake at 325 degrees for 50 minutes or until cheese is lightly brown and pie is set. Yields 1 quiche.

SOMETHING SPECIAL'S ORANGE JUICE GEMS

1 orange
1 cup orange juice
1 stick butter or margarine, softened
1 cup sugar
2 eggs
1 cup chopped pecans
2½ cups sifted flour
2 teaspoons baking powder
½ teaspoon salt
½ teaspoon soda

Quarter the orange and remove the seeds and white pulp. Leave the rind on. Put the orange pieces into a blender with one cup of orange juice and process until the orange is ground up. Set aside. In a separate bowl, cream the butter and sugar thoroughly and beat in the eggs, one at a time. Sift together the flour, baking powder, salt and soda. Add the flour mixture to the creamed butter a third at a time, alternating with the orange juice. Mix well but quickly. Fill small, greased muffin pans two-thirds full and bake at 350 degrees for 20 to 25 minutes. Yields 2 dozen muffins.

IN CLOVER
LaGrange

IN CLOVER

Like the Victorian lady that she is, the house has been sitting sedately for the better part of a century on a tree-lined street in LaGrange. We should all age so gracefully. The house never fell on hard times. She never came down in the world. Built by Leslie Wellington Dallis in 1892 of the very best materials, she serenely raised several generations of Dallises and then became, in her middle years, a restaurant. Her new career suits her well.

The house is now all cream and dusky rose colors. Her Queen Anne cupolas and cubbyholes house marble-top tables and bentwood chairs. The long porch, unobtrusively shielded by thermopane, makes the perfect spot for a rendezvous of the knee-touching variety. There is a pub room in the back, where the thirsty can order victuals to sustain them as they drink. Upstairs are private dining rooms, suitably papered and appointed for a variety of uses.

The food? Exactly what you'd expect from a grande dame of the Old South—only the best, and plenty of it. For lunch you might choose a salad and the Crepes Nantua, filled with creamed shrimp, crabmeat and scallops; or maybe the Crab and Corn Bisque and an Avocado Stuffed with Seafood Salad will petition your taste buds. Dinner could be anything from Chicken in Champagne Sauce to Beef Wellington. You may as well go on and have a piece of that Cheesecake with Raspberry-Cointreau Sauce while you're at it. (If you're dieting, at least order Lace Cookies and take some of them home to share with family and friends. Or, if you have time, make them yourself. We got the recipe for you.) And don't forget to allow time to linger over Irish Coffee. You won't find that task difficult. In Clover is a lingering sort of place.

In Clover is located at 205 Broad Street in LaGrange. Lunch is served Monday through Friday from 11:30 a.m. to 2:00 p.m., and on Saturday from 11:30 a.m. to 2:30 p.m. Dinner is served from 6:00 p.m. to 10:00 p.m. For reservations phone (404) 882-0883.

IN CLOVER'S CRAB AND CORN BISQUE

1 quart seafood stock or bottled clam juice
1 teaspoon thyme leaves
1 teaspoon garlic powder
2 bay leaves
1 teaspoon salt
¼ teaspoon cayenne pepper
1 teaspoon paprika
¼ teaspoon black pepper
¼ teaspoon white pepper
3 drops Tabasco sauce
8 ounces frozen whole-kernel yellow sweet corn
1 stick butter
1 medium onion, diced
2 tablespoons flour
1 pint whipping cream
8 ounces frozen snow crabmeat

Place fish stock in a large saucepan and add all the spices. Bring to a gentle boil, add frozen corn, and simmer for 5 minutes. Meanwhile melt butter in a sauté pan, add the diced onion and sauté until the onions are clear. Stir in the flour and mix with the butter and onions to form a roux. Stir the roux over low heat for 3 minutes. Stir the roux into the soup and simmer gently to thicken it. Add the cream and crabmeat and heat thoroughly, but do not boil. Serve at once. The bisque may be held or reheated in a double boiler. Serves 6.

IN CLOVER'S LACE COOKIES

2 sticks butter (not margarine)
1 pound light brown sugar
2¼ cups quick-cooking oatmeal
3 tablespoons flour
1 teaspoon salt
1 egg, slightly beaten
1 teaspoon vanilla

Melt butter in a 2-quart saucepan. Add the brown sugar, stirring well with a large spoon. Add the remaining ingredients and stir well. Drop by level measuring teaspoonfuls on well-buttered nonstick cookie sheets. Bake at 375 degrees for about 5 minutes. Watch the cookies closely; they should be golden brown. Let cookies cool for 30 seconds and remove with a spatula onto racks to cool completely. If cookies mash together when being removed, they are too warm. If they stick to the pan and break, they are too cool and need to be reheated briefly before removing them from the pan. The cookies can be stored in airtight containers in the freezer. Yields 10 dozen cookies.

Note: Follow the recipe carefully; do not substitute.

IN CLOVER'S ROAST DUCKLING WITH ORANGE-BRANDY SAUCE

Duckling:
- 4 small ducklings
- 2 tablespoons or more lemon juice
- salt to taste
- 4 cups cooked rice
- Orange-Brandy Sauce (recipe follows)
- orange slices for garnish

Buy ducklings weighing about 4 pounds each. (Allow a half a duckling per person.) Rub the skin inside and out with lemon juice, and then salt. Arrange ducks on a rack in an open pan and roast at 350 degrees for about 2 hours. After 30 minutes of cooking and again at the end of the first hour, prick the skin with a sharp fork to allow the fat to drain. To serve, split ducklings in half with a sharp knife and remove the bones from the cavity. Serve over a bed of rice and top with Orange-Brandy Sauce. Garnish with thinly sliced oranges. Serves 8.

Orange-Brandy Sauce:
- 8 ounces frozen orange juice concentrate
- ¾ cup sugar
- ½ cup crushed pineapple
- 4½ cups water
- peel of one orange
- 6 ounces seedless raisins
- 4 tablespoons cornstarch
- 1 ounce brandy

In a large saucepan mix together the orange juice concentrate, sugar, pineapple and 2 cups of the water. Place on low heat. Meanwhile place ½ cup water and the orange peel in a blender and purée. Add the orange peel to the saucepan. Place 1½ cups water in the blender with the raisins and chop coarsely. Add the raisins to the saucepan. Blend the cornstarch into ½ cup water and add to the mixture. Bring to a boil, stirring constantly. Add the brandy and serve hot. The sauce can be made ahead and reheated. It also can be used as a sauce over vanilla ice cream.

OAK TREE RESTAURANT
Hamilton

THE OAK TREE RESTAURANT

I arrived at the Oak Tree Restaurant at dusk and found it all lit up like somebody was having a party. The Oak Tree is a big, white, country-Victorian house, with all the requisite cupolas and shutters, so I figured the restaurant probably serves country-style fare. Inside I found a series of pastel rooms, all with twelve-foot ceilings and Italian marble fireplaces. An enormous, copper cappuccino machine occupies the front hall. When I saw the cappucino machine, I began to suspect that this was not a fried chicken emporium. When I spotted the businesslike rows of wine bottles behind it, and the uniformed bartender standing in front of enough gleaming glass to stock Macy's on a sale day, my suspicions deepened. And when I sat down and looked at the menu, I knew for sure. These people take food very seriously indeed. I was about to enjoy classic continental cuisine and the Someone in the kitchen *wasn't* Dinah. So I checked my wallet surreptitiously to make sure I had my charge cards along, and then I leaned back and enjoyed it.

My husband chose Medallions of Veal with Shrimp, Scallops and Lobster Sauce and murmured sweet nothings to his plate for the rest of the meal. I had escargots and quail, being a purist. The quail arrived looking like a tiny chicken, as I knew it would, and I settled myself down to the tedious but worthwhile task of extracting a meal from it when, lo and behold, it turned out to be boned and stuffed, then cunningly reassembled to look like its former self. Those of you who order quail all the time no doubt expect that sort of trouble to be taken on your behalf. I, who grew up eating buckshot quail, was bowled over. The thing was so beautiful I was reluctant to eat it, but gluttony overcame art.

Good French restaurants affect people that way. There should be a moment of hesitation and wonderment—all this for me?—before you dive in. And there should be a little frivolity, a little surprise, like the one that awaits you when you slice open the Oak Tree's Chicken Duxelle. Or the delight inherent in inverting your first homemade bowlful of Crème Caramel and watching that honey-colored sauce envelop the custard. French cooking is a kind of magic, and the Oak Tree Restaurant has an inordinate number of rabbits in its hat.

The Oak Tree Restaurant is located on Highway 27 in Hamilton. It is open for dinner Monday through Saturday at 6:00 p.m. Reservations are recommended; call (404) 628-4218.

THE OAK TREE RESTAURANT'S CHICKEN DUXELLE

- 4 4-ounce chicken breasts, boned and skinned
- salt and white pepper to taste
- 1 medium onion
- 4 shallot bulbs
- 2 garlic cloves
- 2 cups fresh mushrooms
- ½ ounce good brandy
- 1 cup fresh bread crumbs
- ½ cup chopped parsley
- ½ cup flour, seasoned
- 1 egg
- ½ cup water
- 1 cup chopped pecans
- 1 cup fresh bread crumbs

Pound the chicken breasts between sheets of plastic wrap until they are very thin, like a lace curtain. Season them lightly with salt and white pepper, and refrigerate at least an hour.

To make the duxelle, dice fine the onions, shallots and garlic, and sauté them in butter until golden. Chop and add the mushrooms. Cook until the moisture evaporates and the mixture is light brown. Add the brandy, and cook to evaporate the alcohol. Add just enough bread crumbs to tighten the mix to a paste. Add the parsley. Spread the mushroom paste on the glossy side of each chicken breast, and roll it up jelly-roll fashion, folding in the edges. Refrigerate again for an hour or longer.

Roll each breast in seasoned flour. Blend the egg and water, then dip chicken in the egg wash and roll it in a mixture of the pecans and bread crumbs. Fry in 375-degree deep fat until golden (just a minute or two). Arrange the breasts in a casserole and bake them at 375 degrees for 25 minutes. Serves 4.

THE OAK TREE RESTAURANT'S CREME CARAMEL

Caramel:
2 tablespoons butter **⅓ cup water**
1 cup sugar

Lightly grease 10 custard cups with melted butter. Melt the sugar in water in a small pan, and cook over low heat until amber-colored. Coat the custard cups with the mixture (approximately 1 tablespoon per cup).

Custard:
3 eggs **½ cup sugar**
8 egg yolks **1 teaspoon vanilla**
4 cups milk **pinch of salt**

Preheat oven to 300 degrees. Beat the eggs and yolks with a mixer or whisk until creamy. Scald the milk (do not boil), and add it to the eggs. Add the sugar, vanilla and salt. Pour six ounces of the custard into each cup, and set the cups in a pan, adding some water to the pan to make a water bath for the custard. Bake in a 300-degree oven until set, approximately 1½ hours. To serve, run a knife around the edge of the custard and invert it onto a plate. Serves 10.

BLUDAU'S GOETCHIUS HOUSE
Columbus

BLUDAU'S GOETCHIUS HOUSE

Go to Bludau's Goétchius House expecting knockwurst and beer, and you will be disappointed. Richard Rose Goétchius, who built his house in 1834, was a New Yorker who came south and adopted southern ways to the extent of building this New Orleans-style mansion for his bride. It now sits on the banks of the Chattahoochee River at the end of a row of staunch Federal cottages, like an exuberant wild rose sprouting in a tulip bed. It looks quite natural there, but in truth was chopped into seven pieces and relocated on the spot some twenty years ago.

While you dine, you can entertain yourself wondering where the mansion was cut and how the people who cut it ever put it back together. It's an enormous, wandering place, with many little dining rooms leading into other dining rooms. Downstairs is a dark, wonderful bar. Outside is a patio with a fountain. You can even eat on the back porch if you like. The décor is "New Orleans Victorian," with gold curtains and lots of roses in the carpets. The menu is large and varied, and at lunch there's a buffet if you're in a hurry.

A typical dinner might begin with the hors d'oeuvres sampler—Oysters Rockefeller, Clams Casino, Escargots Duxelles, Frog Legs Bourgouignone and Stuffed Mushrooms. In fact, it might end there, and quite happily, but then you'd miss getting to choose between fresh Red Snapper Française, Chicken Terrine with Pâté and Steak Diane. To finish, try Bananas Foster. Or pick a wedge from the cake cart. I picked three wedges, amazing my friends and relations, and fought my son for the last bite of Lemon Cake. He won, being only three and not averse to screaming to make a point.

The most pleasant thing about the Goétchius House, besides the food and the house itself, is the feeling that if your three-year-old son did decide to throw a massive fit in the middle of dinner, no one would care. A waiter would probably come over and make faces at him until he forgot to be unhappy. In case you don't have children, let me explain. There are many restaurants serving good food, many historic restaurants and many restaurants tolerant of children, but all three attributes are rarely found in the *same* restaurant. The Goétchius House is such a restaurant.

Bludau's Goétchius House is located at 405 Broadway in Columbus. Lunch and a buffet are served from 11:30 a.m. until 2:00 p.m. Monday through Friday. Dinner is served from 6:00 p.m. until 10:45 p.m. Monday through Saturday. Reservations for dinner are strongly recommended; call (404) 324-4863. The Goétchius House is closed all day Sunday.

BLUDAU'S GOETCHIUS HOUSE'S
GARLIC BUTTER

small bunch of scallions
¼ cup Burgundy
2 sticks butter
2 sticks margarine
1 teaspoon ground cloves
½ onion, chopped
2 garlic cloves, minced
¼ cup fresh parsley, chopped
¼ cup shallots

Chop the scallions and boil them in a small amount of Burgundy until the Burgundy is evaporated. In a food processor, whip the butter and margarine. Add the other ingredients and process until whipped and very fluffy. Yields 2¼ cups.

Note: Garlic Butter can be frozen in tablespoon-size lumps and added to any sautéed fish.

BLUDAU'S GOETCHIUS HOUSE'S
VEAL NATUREL

1 pound veal tenderloin, hand-sliced
dash of thyme
dash of lemon juice
salt and pepper to taste
flour for dredging
2 tablespoons butter
2 tablespoons oil
½ pound mushrooms, sliced
10 scallions, chopped
¼ to ½ cup cream sherry

Sprinkle the veal slices with thyme, lemon juice, salt and pepper, and marinate for several hours in the refrigerator. Flour the pieces lightly and sauté, a few at a time, in the butter and oil until brown. Remove veal from the pan and keep it warm. Add more butter to the pan, if needed, and sauté the mushrooms and scallions until glazed. Then add cream sherry, cover the pan and simmer for a minute. Pour sauce over the veal and, if desired, serve with rissolé potatoes. Serves 2 to 4.

BLUDAU'S GOETCHIUS HOUSE'S
RED SNAPPER FRANCAISE

1 fresh snapper, filleted
salt and pepper to taste
¼ teaspoon thyme
¼ teaspoon Hungarian
   paprika
1 egg
1 teaspoon fresh parsley,
   minced
½ teaspoon Parmesan and
   Romano cheese mix
1 tablespoon butter
1 tablespoon oil
flour for dredging
1 tablespoon garlic butter
   (recipe above)
dash of sherry

Cut the fish fillet into three or so pieces and season it with salt, pepper, thyme and paprika. In a shallow bowl, stir together the egg, parsley and cheeses. In a frying pan, melt the butter with the oil on medium-low heat until hot. Coat the fish pieces with flour and dip them into the egg mix, then into the frying pan. Sauté until golden brown on the bottom, then turn them over and add Garlic Butter and a splash of sherry to the pan. Sauté until done, and serve immediately. Serves 1 to 2.

THE RANKIN QUARTER
Columbus

THE RANKIN QUARTER

Back in the 1880s when Columbus was a busy river port, the Rankin Hotel was, I imagine, a handy place for travelers to spend the night before boarding a steamboat south to the Gulf. It was large, square and brick, and it stood a convenient two blocks from the Chattahoochee, providing a bed and victuals to all passersby. It also had the distinction of being the first hotel in town with indoor bathrooms. Bathrooms are of course commonplace now, and a bed at the Rankin is no longer a possibility, but the old place is once again feeding people in style and comfort.

The downstairs, which once housed a newsstand and grocery store, has been stripped down to the original brick. The windows are wide, curving arches, some of which look out upon an interior courtyard. It's a comfortable, airy, no-nonsense sort of place, where lots of different types of people feel at home. Business people can get a quick bite and talk over a deal or linger by the lovely Victorian bar and sip a libation. Couples and tourists can relax over maps and conversation. Tired mothers can take a table along the banquette which runs down one wall and prop their babies beside them as they eat.

During my last visit I sat in a corner and watched just such an assortment rush in, along with about two hundred of their friends, and they were all served and happily eating in about fifteen minutes. The owners, Frankie Freed and Janie Saine believe in giving people value for their money. Parading by, there were steaming soups and fresh-looking salads, luscious sandwiches and, that day, plates and plates of lasagne, the daily special. The menu features deli fare, including a "Create Your Own" sandwich, and daily specials, announced on a chalkboard in the foyer.

In her spare time, Saine is restoring the old hotel stable as a club, to be called the Livery. And she has plans to begin serving dinner at the Rankin Quarter soon. From the looks of the lunch crowd, tomorrow would not be too soon for the citizens of Columbus.

The Rankin Quarter is located at 21 Tenth Street in Columbus, two blocks north of the restoration area. Lunch is served Monday through Friday from 11:00 a.m. until 3:00 p.m. Reservations are not necessary, but the phone number is (404) 322-8151.

THE RANKIN QUARTER'S
BANANA FLUFF

Crust:
1 cup self-rising flour
½ cup chopped pecans
1 stick butter, melted

Combine the ingredients for the crust and press out into an 8 ½-by-11-inch baking dish. Bake at 350 degrees in a preheated oven for 20 minutes. Allow crust to cool.

Filling:
8 ounces soft cream cheese
½ cup confectioners' sugar
7 ounces instant vanilla pudding mix
2 cups milk
1 8-ounce package Cool Whip
2 bananas

In a large bowl, cream with a mixer the cream cheese and confectioners' sugar. Add the pudding mix, milk and Cool Whip; beat well. On the cool crust, put a layer of sliced bananas; top with the pudding mixture. Cover and refrigerate overnight. Serves 6 to 8.

THE RANKIN QUARTER'S
HAM DELITE

1 cup sliced fresh mushrooms
1 small onion
2 tablespoons butter
2 tablespoons cooking sherry
1 English muffin
1 tablespoon mayonnaise
3 ounces sliced ham
2 slices tomato
2 slices Swiss cheese

Sauté mushrooms and onions over low heat for 15 to 20 minutes in butter and cooking sherry. Remove from heat. Split muffin and spread each side with mayonnaise. Pile on sliced ham and top with sautéed vegetables, tomato slices and Swiss cheese. Heat in a microwave oven for 1½ minutes on high, until cheese melts. Or heat in a 400-degree oven until the cheese melts. Serves 1.

THE RANKIN QUARTER'S GRAMMY'S BAKED BEANS

¼ pound bacon, chopped
1 medium onion, chopped
1 2-pound can pork and beans
½ cup light brown sugar
½ teaspoon liquid smoke
1 tablespoon Worcestershire sauce

2 tablespoons Gulden's mustard
2 tablespoons catsup
2 tablespoons sweet salad cube pickles
1½ tablespoons light corn syrup

Brown together in a frying pan the chopped bacon and onions. Meanwhile, in a baking pan combine the rest of the ingredients. Add the browned bacon and onions, and bake at 350 degrees for 1 to 1½ hours. Serves 10 to 12.

THE FARMHOUSE
Ellerslie

THE FARMHOUSE

The first time I saw the Farmhouse, there was a line of people standing patiently outside, waiting to eat lunch. Since the Farmhouse is several miles from anywhere and down a dirt road at that, I was intrigued and sauntered over to the end of the line to wait with them. There was a half-acre of Cadillacs, Mercedeses, Volkswagons and flat-bed trucks parked around in the yard—like a wake. No one was sad, though, or even surly. Everyone was laughing and talking and having a good time. No one looked at his watch.

"This place must be really something," I ventured.

"Well . . . we like it."

"What's good to eat?"

"Oh, everything. Everything is quite good."

Once inside I discovered that, though the Farmhouse is very clean and rustic, no effort has been made to preserve the house for its own sake. Nobody famous ever lived there, and it's not architecturally important except, perhaps, in this one significant respect—its very ordinariness. The house was built around 1900 for tenants or sharecroppers, and it is typical of the plain, no-frills life they led.

When my food arrived, I finally knew why everyone in the line was grinning. Lunch was wonderful. Not pig-out wonderful, like an all-you-can-eat place. Not greasy wonderful, like a fish house. Not elegantly wonderful, like an uptown dining spot. Just plain, ordinary good. There was the perfect Meat Loaf, a delicious Squash Casserole, mouth-watering Sour Cream Cornbread, really good Iced Tea, the Coconut Cake I've been looking for all my life. All the cakes are delectable—Caramel Layer Cake, Brown Sugar Cake and Lemon-Pineapple Layer Cake are all temptations that test a dieter's resolve.

"We started this place six years ago as an outlet for our crafts," said the owners. "We had two tables, and we brought mom out here to cook for us. It just grew. Now we serve two or three hundred people a weekend." The mom referred to is

Katie Osborne, and she makes all the food herself. It's no wonder the lines are so long.

The Farmhouse is found on Route 1 in Ellerslie, off Highway 85 North. It is open for lunch on Friday and Saturday from 11:30 a.m. to 2:00 p.m. No reservations are necessary. Special arrangements can be made for lunch or dinner for a party of fifteen or more. Call (404) 561-3435.

THE FARMHOUSE'S COCONUT CAKE

1 cup unsalted butter (not margarine)
2 cups sugar
4 eggs
½ teaspoon salt
1 tablespoon vanilla
1 teaspoon soda
1½ cups buttermilk
3 cups plain flour

Cream the butter and sugar. Add unbeaten eggs, one at a time, beating with a mixer after each addition. Add salt and vanilla. Stir soda into the buttermilk. To the first mixture add about a half a cup of the flour, then some of the buttermilk, beating after each addition. Continue adding the ingredients, alternating until the buttermilk and flour are gone. Grease three 8-inch cake pans and cut waxed paper to fit the bottoms. Divide the batter among the pans, shake it down and bake at 350 degrees for 20 minutes or until the cake tests done. Cool the layers for 10 minutes and then remove them from the pans, leaving the waxed paper stuck to the cake. Stack the layers on top of each other and cover with a light towel overnight or until completely cold. Then take the layers apart, removing the waxed paper and rolling with fingers any remaining brown particles that remain on the cake, so that there is no crust on the tops of the layers. Frost, and store in the refrigerator for a day or two before eating. Yields 1 cake.

Frosting:
3 cups sugar
1½ cups milk
2 9-ounce packages frozen coconut, defrosted
1 stick unsalted butter
1 teaspoon vanilla

Cook the sugar and milk together for about 10 minutes after liquid has begun to boil. Add the coconut and reduce heat. Continue cooking more slowly until mixture changes color slightly, from a real white to an oyster white. Remove from heat, add butter and vanilla and stir well. Let frosting cool to lukewarm and spread it between the layers and on top of the cake. It will seep down into the cake and make it very moist and good.

THE FARMHOUSE'S STIR-FRY CABBAGE

½ cabbage
1 small onion
1 bell pepper
2 stalks celery
2 fresh tomatoes

salt and pepper to taste
½ to 1 teaspoon sugar
1 tablespoon oil
1 tablespoon butter or margarine

Chop the cabbage into strips and cut up the other vegetables. Peel and chop the tomato. Sprinkle the vegetables with salt, pepper and sugar. Heat the oil and butter in a large frying pan or wok and add the vegetables, cooking for 2 minutes. Then cook for 2 more minutes with a lid on. Serves 6.

THE FARMHOUSE'S SOUR CREAM CORNBREAD

1½ cups self-rising cornmeal
2 tablespoons sugar
2 eggs
½ cup cooking oil

1 cup cream-style corn, fresh or frozen
1 medium onion, chopped
1 cup sour cream

Mix all ingredients well. Grease large muffin tins, and pour them about ¾ full of batter. Bake at 400 degrees for 20 to 25 minutes. Serve hot. Yields 16 to 18 muffins.

THE VICTORIAN TEA ROOM
Warm Springs

VICTORIAN TEA ROOM

In the 1920s Warm Springs was a sleepy little resort town sitting on the railroad tracks in the middle of Georgia. Folks came to stay at the Meriweather Hotel and bathe at the springs, hoping to cure what ailed them or at least pass the time pleasantly. Among the hopefuls was a young New York lawyer who had been cruelly stricken with polio in 1921 and could not seem to recover either the use of his legs or his zest for life. After his visit to the springs the man was so impressed with his improvement that he bought the hotel and started a hospital there. Then he went home and became governor of New York and, in 1932, president of the United States. Franklin Delano Roosevelt and Warm Springs thus established the mutually beneficial association that was to continue until Roosevelt's death there in 1945. Throughout the trials of his tenure as a four-term, wartime president, Roosevelt would periodically retreat to his home in Warm Springs for rejuvenation.

Now Warm Springs itself is undergoing a kind of rejuvenation, as the cars and tour buses roll in on their way to the Little White House and Callaway Gardens. The village, which after Roosevelt's death became a virtual ghost town, is now a thriving tourist mecca, filled with an assortment of shops offering antiques, crafts and memorabilia. And when one tires of sightseeing, there is the Victorian Tea Room, built in 1906 as Talbot's General Mercantile. I could find no evidence that Franklin or Eleanor ever wandered into the mercantile to buy a paper and chat with the locals, but I imagine they did, and you are welcome to the same fantasy if it pleases you.

You won't need a fantasy to spice up your lunch because the food here is plenty good enough to stand on its own. You can choose a meat and three vegetables or order a sandwich or salad from the menu. If you are there on a Friday night, you can partake with local patrons in a buffet dinner, either country or seafood.

Don't be deceived, as I was, by the "Victorian" and "Tea" portions of the restaurant's name. That phraseology always connotes to me an abundance of discomfort and very little to eat. Happily, such is not the case here.

The Victorian Tea Room is located on Main Street in Warm Springs. Lunch is served Tuesday through Saturday from 11:30 a.m. until 3:00 p.m., Sunday buffet is from 11:30 a.m. until 3:00 p.m. Dinner is served on Friday evenings from 5:30 until 9:00—a seafood buffet on the first and third Fridays of the month. Reservations are recommended for large groups. Call (404) 655-2319.

VICTORIAN TEA ROOM'S
SEAFOOD BROCCOLI CASSEROLE

1 10-ounce package frozen broccoli spears
1 pound raw shrimp, peeled and deveined (or crabmeat, sealegs or fish)
1 can cream of shrimp soup
1 cup mayonnaise
1 tablespoon lemon juice
1 tablespoon margarine
½ cup grated Cheddar cheese
dash of paprika

Prepare the broccoli by boiling it according to package directions in salted water until tender. Drain it and lay the stalks in a shallow casserole. Top with the shrimp or other seafood. Prepare a sauce by mixing all the remaining ingredients together in a saucepan (reserving some cheese for topping) and stirring over low heat until the cheese and margarine melt. (If the sauce seems too thick, dilute it with a little warm water.) Pour the sauce over the seafood and broccoli; sprinkle with the leftover cheese and a dash of paprika. Bake at 350 degrees until the shrimp has turned pink, 20 to 30 minutes. Serves 4.

THE VICTORIAN TEA ROOM'S
SQUASH CASSEROLE

6 to 8 medium yellow squash
1 medium onion
2 beaten eggs
3 tablespoons margarine
2 tablespoons pimientos
½ bell pepper, chopped
1 cup mayonnaise
cayenne pepper to taste
salt to taste
1¼ cups mild Cheddar cheese, grated

Slice the squash and chop the onion; simmer them together with a little water until tender, 10 to 15 minutes. Drain excess water, and stir in the other ingredients, reserving ¼ cup of cheese. Pour the mixture into a greased casserole, sprinkle with the reserved cheese, and bake at 350 degrees for 20 minutes or until firm. Serves 6.

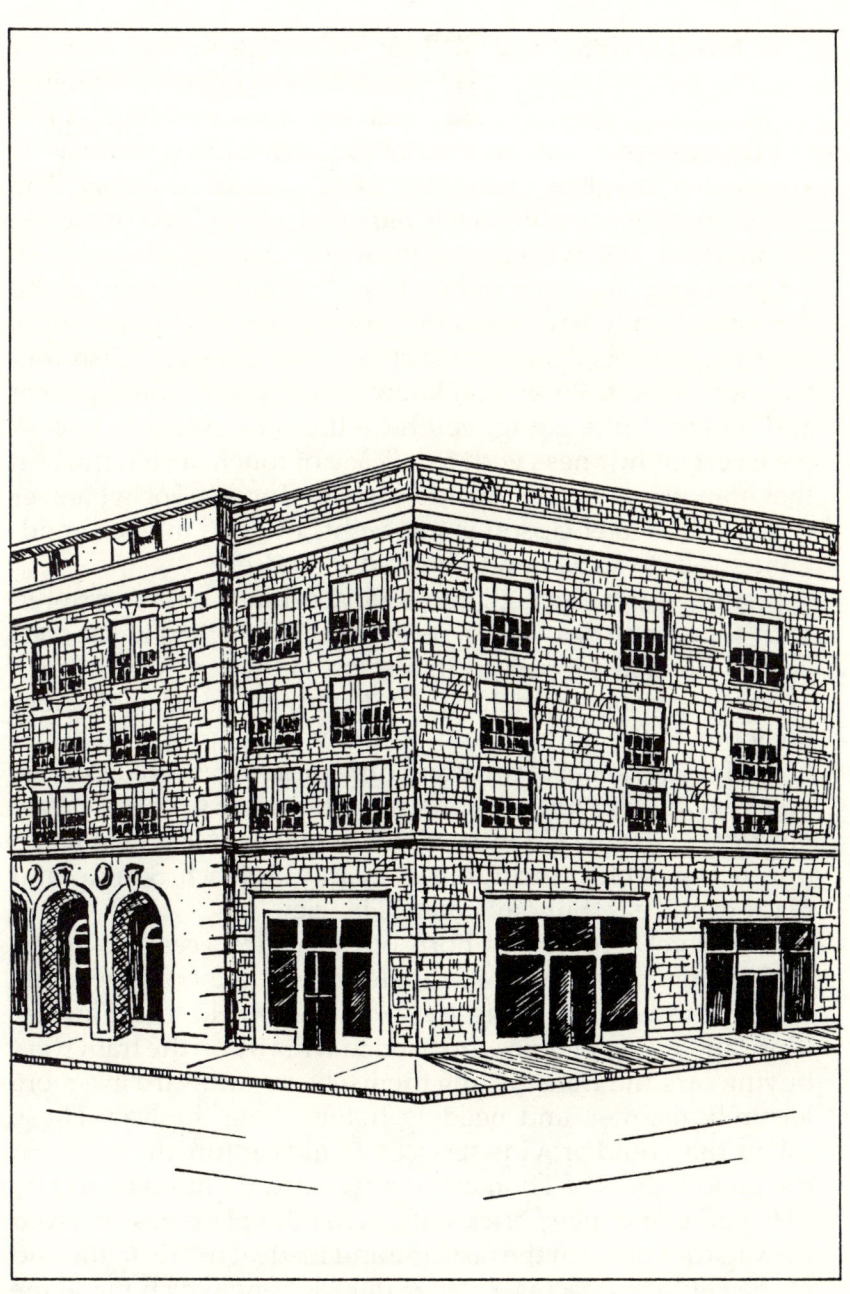

THE HOTEL UPSON
Thomaston

THE HOTEL UPSON The Hotel Upson will surprise you. It is neither a crumbling relic nor a restored relic. It will not depress you with an aura of faded grandeur or unsettle you with a too-glossy patina covering God knows what. The Hotel Upson is merely a lovely old hotel, owned and managed by Bill Andrews, who grew up there because his father John Andrews was manager before him. Seven generations of the Andrews family have lived in Upson County. Perhaps that's why the hotel looks so comfortable and has such fresh and wonderful food. When you know where you're coming from and where you're going, you have the self-assurance to couple a certain firmness with a delicacy of touch, a combination that sometimes eludes wandering developers. For whatever reason, the Hotel Upson is just right, from its mustard-and-white walls to its Seafood Thermidor Andrews.

Visitors enter through the lobby, a huge room scattered with sofas and rugs, with a reception desk tucked in the back corner. Breakfast is served in a room to the left, which has a separate entrance from the street. For lunch, go straight across the lobby to the dining room, where you can procure a buffet lunch for a reasonable price and dine under brass chandeliers. Weekday lunch typically consists of Boneless Chicken Breast Supreme, Georgia Country Ham, Barbecue, Meat Loaf and a dozen vegetables, including a creamy Spinach Soufflé and Black-eyed Peas. Sunday lunch is fancier.

The Hotel Upson was born out of civic necessity. In the 1920s Thomaston found itself, along with a lot of other little Georgia towns, standing between the world and Florida. More and more, people who used to whiz by on the train were buying cars and transporting themselves southward in a more leisurely manner, and needing hotels along the way. Those towns that could provide services would capture the trade. So the good fathers of Thomaston organized themselves and by 1928 had a fine, new, brick hotel. That the place has survived the vagaries of life in the fast lane and made it nearly to the end of the century intact is a minor miracle, one which made me want to do a small dance of thanksgiving in the lobby. But I restrained myself.

You will understand my joy if you grew up, as I did, going to the local hotel on Sundays for lunch with your family, meeting your friends there, perhaps playing a discreet game of hide-and-seek in the lobby while your parents argued politics and your grandmother told you to keep away from those nasty spittoons. Occasionally, if you were lucky, a stranger who was actually staying there would give you a nickel and call you a cute child, while your aunts eyed him suspiciously from the next sofa. If you were denied such worldly pleasures as a child, consider paying the Hotel Upson a visit some day soon. After all, it's never too late for a treat.

The Hotel Upson is located at 200 South Church Street in Thomaston. Breakfast is served from 7:00 a.m. until 11:00 a.m. Monday through Sunday except Saturday. A buffet lunch is served Monday through Friday from 11:00 a.m. until 2:00 p.m., and on Sunday there is a smorgasbord from noon until 2:00 p.m. The dining room is open on occasional Friday nights, by reservation only. Call (404) 647-7126.

THE HOTEL UPSON'S
SEAFOOD THERMIDOR ANDREWS

1 stick butter or margarine
2 cups chopped onions
2 cups chopped bell peppers
2 cups chopped celery
2½ cups sliced mushrooms
2 to 3 cups medium shrimp, peeled and deveined
1 pound lump, white crabmeat
1 pound bay scallops, uncooked
1 pint cooking sherry
1 quart half-and-half
4 tablespoons cornstarch
1 cup water
½ to ¾ cup grated Parmesan or Romano cheese
dash of paprika

Melt the butter in a large skillet and sauté the onions, peppers and celery until almost done, being careful not to burn the onions. Add mushrooms, shrimp, crabmeat and scallops, and continue to cook slowly until the shrimp turns pink. Douse the cooking sherry over entire ingredients while still cooking; then add the half-and-half. Do not allow the mixture to boil at any time. If you need more liquid to make sufficient sauce, add some more cream or a little whole milk. Stir several tablespoons of cornstarch into a cup of water, making a fairly thick paste; then stir this very slowly into the thermidor mixture to thicken it. Do not add the cornstarch all at once; add only what is necessary to get the consistency you desire.

Put the seafood mixture into a large casserole dish and sprinkle it generously with grated cheese. Put a dash of paprika on top of the cheese to add color. (If you're not ready to serve the dish, refrigerate it.) Place the dish in a 350-degree oven and bake until the cheese bubbles around the edges, usually about 30 to 40 minutes. Serves 6 to 8 generously.

THE HOTEL UPSON'S FRIED CHICKEN

2 teaspoons salt
½ teaspoon pepper
1 package Ranch dressing mix
1 pint buttermilk
3 eggs
2 cups unsifted flour
2½- to 3-pound chicken, cut into 8 pieces
1 quart Wesson oil

Mix the salt, pepper and dressing mix together; then divide into two equal portions. Make a batter of the buttermilk, eggs and half the salt, pepper and Ranch dressing mix. Mix the remaining seasonings into the flour. Soak the chicken parts in the milk mix. Then roll them in flour until coated. Fry in hot oil about 20 minutes or until done, turning once. Using enough oil to half-cover the chicken will ensure that it cooks quickly and thoroughly. Serves 4.

THE HOTEL UPSON'S SPINACH SOUFFLE

2 10-ounce packages frozen chopped spinach
1 pint sour cream
1 teaspoon garlic salt
3 drops red hot sauce

Cook spinach according to package directions and drain. Fold in sour cream, garlic salt and hot sauce. Heat in a 350-degree oven for 10 to 15 minutes or in the microwave until hot. Serves 5 to 6.

THE LEFT BANQUE
Forsyth

THE LEFT BANQUE

In 1908 you could have stood on the square in Forsyth on a Saturday morning and seen much the same thing that you can see there now. The Monroe County Courthouse sat smack in the middle of the square, a proud testament to the county's progressive outlook. On the courthouse lawn, the obligatory Confederate monument had just been unveiled. The place would have been bustling with folks who had come to town to do business at the cotton exchange or the brokerage office, or to spend their money at one of the stores which lined the square. There were no sidewalks then, and you might have had to pick your way around bales of cotton stacked up awaiting shipment and teams and wagons parked haphazardly along the road. As you sauntered along Johnston Street, you would have remembered that Joel Chandler Harris used to sit in a building on that corner and compose stories. On the next corner was the town's newest bank, with Forsyth Mercantile conveniently next door. The mercantile was partitioned and had two separate entrances for shoppers—one for men and one for women, on the theory, presumably, that members of either sex would rather shop for their BVD's or corsets in comparative privacy.

Now the cotton bales and horses are gone, but the mercantile and bank are still there, having been transformed into a bar and restaurant called the Left Banque, with an adjoining series of snappy little shops. You can go there and reminisce over lunch. A cafe bar facing the street offers an opportunity for more spontaneous thirst-quenching, as well.

The building's restorers have kept, where possible, the wide-plank flooring and decorative motifs which originally characterized the place, adding such touches as murals, a carousel horse, antique leaded windows from England and, quite curiously, lampposts from Macon's old Second Street Bridge. It's a perfect lunch layover if you're traveling up or down I-75, and as a bonus you can sample for yourself a Cream of Broccoli Soup that is the best I've ever tested or ever hope to taste. The Mandarin Orange Salad is also a knockout, and I've included both recipes for you.

The Left Banque is on the Square, on Johnston Street, in Forsyth. Lunch is served Tuesday through Saturday from 11:30 a.m. until 2:30 p.m.; dinner is served Friday and Saturday from 6:00 p.m. to 9:00 p.m. For reservations call (912) 994-5505.

THE LEFT BANQUE'S
CREAM OF BROCCOLI SOUP

4 cups chicken broth
1 10-ounce package frozen chopped broccoli
2 medium onions, chopped
1 stick butter
½ cup flour
4 cups milk
½ cup cream or half-and-half
salt and pepper to taste

In a medium saucepan, heat the chicken broth and add the frozen broccoli and chopped onions. Simmer, uncovered, for 20 to 30 minutes while preparing the rest of the soup. In a small sauté pan, melt the butter and add the flour, stirring over low heat for 3 or 4 minutes to make a roux. Let the roux cool to room temperature. Meanwhile, heat the milk in a large saucepan and add the cool roux, stirring with a whisk for 4 or 5 minutes. The mixture will be quite thick. When the broccoli-onion broth is ready, stir it gradually into the thickened milk. If the soup seems to be getting too thin, reserve some of the broth. Add about half a cup of cream or half-and-half, and season with salt and pepper. Serves 4 to 6.

THE LEFT BANQUE'S
SOY SAUCE DRESSING

¼ cup water
½ cup soy sauce
3 tablespoons sugar
3 tablespoons vinegar
½ teaspoon garlic salt
½ cup oil

Mix all the ingredients together, and store in refrigerator. Use on spinach salad. Yields approximately 2 cups.

THE LEFT BANQUE'S
MANDARIN ORANGE SALAD

Salad:
- 4 large lettuce leaves
- 2 cups mandarin orange slices
- 4 tablespoons toasted almond slivers

To serve, arrange each serving on a separate salad plate. Place a lettuce leaf on each plate and cover with a mound of mandarin orange slices and a sprinkle of toasted almond slivers. Cover with dressing. The dressing is good on any fruit salad. Serves 4.

Dressing:
- ¼ cup orange juice concentrate
- ¼ cup sugar
- 3 tablespoons lemon juice
- 3 tablespoons sweet vermouth
- 3 tablespoons vinegar
- ¾ cup oil

Mix all ingredients well. Store extra dressing in refrigerator.

BEALL'S 1860
Macon

BEALL'S 1860

Not only was cotton king of the South, but wealthy planters like Nathan Beall built homes fit for a king. During the 1850s, Beall was bringing cotton from his Jones County plantation into Macon to be shipped via the Ocmulgee River to Savannah. He became so enchanted by Macon's social life that he decided to build a home there as well. It took Beall from 1855 to 1860 to complete this Italian Renaissance home. Unfortunately, the Bealls were able to enjoy their dream only a short time due to General Sherman's march to the sea. When his Jones County plantation was destroyed and the Union occupied Macon, Beall was forced to sell his town home to the Stevens family.

Ten years later, the house was sold once again, this time to the Jordan family. The first Mrs. Jordan took great pride in running her new home with style. In fact, she felt such attachment that, it is said, her spirit often materialized at the top of the stairway in the years immediately following her death. This was not exactly the reception that Mr. Jordan had planned for his second wife, but the first Mrs. Jordan was soon spotted by his new bride.

In the 1900s, the new owner, Judge Dunlap, made extensive structural changes by removing the cupola and rounded roof and adding tin columns to three sides, transforming the facade to Greek Revival. He also created the two-story vaulted foyer, which makes an impressive entrance. I had lunch in the adjoining room with my friend Becky Aliff and Lillyan Hanberry, who is a co-owner.

The restaurant is known for its Chicken Sweet & Hot, which is served with a slightly sweet sauce that has the overtones of a spicy barbecue sauce. Becky ordered their Crabmeat Benedict, which, with its piquant freshness, was a creative approach to a traditional dish. Since our visit was shortly before Thanksgiving, Hanberry gave me a taste of their old-fashioned Turkey Dressing, which later became an instant pleaser to my family.

We toured the upstairs and downstairs dining rooms and saw the remnants of rough, dark paneling that was added by a Canadian family to remind them of their country. The barrel-vaulted main dining room was quite impressive with its large salad bar occupying the spot where the Dunlap's china cabinet once stood. It was here that we decided to sample the Lemon Squares and Chocolate Walnut Pie, and we soon realized that these desserts required a redefinition of the word *sampling*. Since the spirit of the former Mrs. Jordan has not been seen or heard from in some time, I assume that she is well pleased with the tasty adaptation of her stately home. I certainly am.

Beall's 1860 is located at 315 College Street in Macon. Meals are served from 11:30 a.m. until 10:30 p.m. Monday through Saturday. For reservations (desired) call (912) 745-3663.

BEALL'S LEMON SQUARES

Crust:
1 cup butter, melted
2 cups all-purpose flour, sifted
½ cup confectioners' sugar

Preheat oven to 350 degrees. In a mixing bowl, combine above ingredients and mix until blended. Butter a 9-by-13-by-2-inch pan and pat mixture evenly into bottom of pan. Bake for 15 minutes.

Topping:
2 cups sugar
4 tablespoons all-purpose flour
1 teaspoon baking powder
4 eggs
6 tablespoons lemon juice
pinch of salt
confectioners' sugar for garnish

With electric mixer, blend sugar, flour and baking powder. Add eggs, one at a time, beating after each addition; then add lemon juice and salt. Pour over hot crust and bake in a 350-degree oven for 20 to 25 minutes. Cool, sprinkle with confectioners' sugar, and cut into squares. Yields 4 dozen.

BEALL'S TURKEY DRESSING

3 cups turkey or chicken stock
1 cup cornmeal
1 large onion, grated
2 large eggs, lightly beaten
1 cup bread crumbs
salt and pepper to taste
½ cup pecans, broken
½ pint or more oysters (optional)

In a large saucepan over low heat, pour 1½ cups stock and stir in cornmeal until lumps are dissolved. Add onions, stirring to combine. Add eggs and stir until mixed. Alternately add bread crumbs and remaining stock. Salt and pepper to taste and cook very slowly for 45 minutes or longer, stirring occasionally. Add pecans and oysters and cook until flavored through. Serves 12.

BEALL'S CHICKEN SWEET & HOT

1 stick butter
¼ cup Worcestershire sauce
1 clove garlic, minced
½ cup red currant jelly
1 tablespoon Dijon mustard
1 cup orange juice
1 teaspoon powdered ginger
3 dashes of Tabasco sauce
8 chicken breasts, skinned and deboned

In a small saucepan over simmering heat, combine all ingredients except chicken. Stir until jelly is melted and sauce is smooth. Cool. Pour sauce over chicken and marinate in refrigerator for 3 hours. Place chicken and marinade in a broiler pan and cook at 350 degrees, about 8 or 9 inches below the broiler unit. Bake for about 45 minutes, turning and basting periodically. Serves 8.

NEW PERRY HOTEL AND MOTEL
Perry

NEW PERRY HOTEL AND MOTEL

There's an old saying that claims a person "can get more with honey than with vinegar." During the Civil War, the women of Perry took that adage to heart when Union troops camped near their homes. In order to put a different face on southern social patterns, these wise ladies and their children took buttermilk and cookies to the soldiers in their camp. However, one of the soldiers not only took the food from two young boys, but their horse as well. When the boys' mother learned of their mistreatment, she gave the camp officer a vinegary tongue-lashing that resulted in the return of the horse. Overall, though, it is believed that the women's simple act of kindness saved Perry from being burned and pillaged, as were so many other neighboring areas.

Had the Union soldiers broken camp and ventured into Perry, they would probably have been a sight more comfortable at Cox's Inn, built of wood in 1850 as a stagecoach stop. Twenty-some years later, when the railroad was extended into Perry, the finer Perry Hotel was built on this site. After that building was razed in 1924, what is now known as the New Perry Hotel was erected the following year. It was to this venerable old establishment that I arrived a little late for dinner. Owners Mr. and Mrs. Yates Green and their partner, Harold Green, could have told me that the dining room was closed and I would have understood, but instead that old Perry hospitality emerged.

An hour later, we sat in the main dining room and talked as I devoured very moist, pan-broiled chicken, a helping of Macaroni and Cheese and a truly excellent Cornbread Dressing. While I was traveling through Georgia, other restaurateurs had suggested that I try New Perry's Shredded Yams and their Broccoli Casserole. The yams weren't available that evening, but the broccoli with its rich cheese and herb dressing was wonderfully southern. While in the center of peach country, I wasn't about to pass up their Peach Pan Pie, and I quickly understood why people pull off the interstate year after year for a slice.

At breakfast the next morning, the Greens and I dined in their Garden Dining Room, which was filled with fresh camellias from their garden. It was a country breakfast of fresh fruit, country ham, biscuits, sausage, eggs and salt pork. I learned that salt pork was once called sawmill steak. This meat was popular because it was affordable for mill workers and didn't require refrigeration—quite an advantage at a time when few people owned iceboxes. Then, just when I thought I couldn't swallow another delicious bite, they surprised me with a batch of Shredded Yams. They didn't want me to come so far and be disappointed, so the cook made a fresh, yummy batch that morning. Now that's what I mean by Perry hospitality!

The New Perry Hotel and Motel is located at 800 Main Street in Perry. Breakfast is served from 7:00 a.m. until 10:00 a.m.; lunch from 11:30 a.m. until 2:30 p.m.; and dinner from 5:30 p.m. until 9:00 p.m., daily. For reservations (accepted, but not required) call (912) 987-1000.

NEW PERRY HOTEL'S SHREDDED YAMS

2 pounds sweet potatoes, raw
1 gallon water
1 tablespoon salt
1 cup sugar
½ cup white Karo syrup
½ cup water
¼ cup margarine
1 cup pineapple juice

Preheat oven to 350 degrees. Peel and shred potatoes in a grinder or with the shredder in a food processor or with a hand grater. Place in a gallon of water. Add salt. Drain and wash well. Place potatoes in a 11½-by-7½-inch buttered baking dish. In a medium saucepan, mix sugar, Karo syrup and ½ cup water. Cook over medium heat until it becomes a simple syrup. Add margarine. Pour pineapple juice over potatoes, then add syrup. Bake 35 minutes or until potatoes are transparent. Serves 12.

NEW PERRY HOTEL'S PEACH PAN PIE

1 recipe pie crust dough, prepared
3 cups sliced fresh peaches
1 cup sugar
¼ cup water
2 to 3 tablespoons butter
2 to 3 tablespoons all-purpose flour

Set aside half of pie dough in refrigerator. Roll out remaining half in a circle. Fit dough into bottom of an 8-inch pie plate and prick bottom with a fork. Slice peaches to a medium thickness. In a medium saucepan, add sugar and water and bring to a boil. Boil for a few seconds. Add peaches and simmer for about 10 minutes. Form layer of peaches in bottom of pie crust, dot with cubes of butter and sprinkle evenly with flour. Repeat procedure until all peaches are used. Roll out remaining pie crust and place over top of peaches, crimping sides with a fork to seal. Cut slits in the top of pie. Bake in a preheated 350-degree oven for 30 to 40 minutes until the crust is light brown. Yields 1 pie.

NEW PERRY HOTEL'S BROCCOLI CASSEROLE

2 10-ounce packages frozen broccoli
3 to 4 tablespoons butter
1 cup herb-flavored bread stuffing (commercial)
1 can cream of mushroom soup
1 cup grated Cheddar cheese
¼ cup milk
1 teaspoon grated onions
dash of salt

Preheat oven to 350 degrees. Cook broccoli according to package directions and drain. Butter a 1½- to 2-quart casserole dish. In a mixing bowl, combine all ingredients and spread evenly in casserole. Bake for 30 minutes. Serves 6.

SUSINA PLANTATION INN
Thomasville

SUSINA PLANTATION INN The soft patter of rain through the mossy, live oaks, the occasional caw of a blackbird and the creaking of my old wicker swing were the only sounds that broke the silence on Susina's upstairs porch. It was in 1840 when James and Harriet Blackshear built this Greek Revival, white-columned mansion, and if I hadn't noticed a telephone pole before winding up the dirt path to the plantation, I wouldn't have known I was in this century.

And neither does the spirit of Mrs. Blackshear, who, it is said, "takes death as a mere inconvenience" in the routine of overseeing her home. Widowed with five young children and the task of producing two hundred and thirty-five bales of cotton, Mrs. Blackshear became a rather remarkable figure in her day, winning the respect of her contemporaries. So, it is understandable that she didn't want to lose this public esteem after her death. Though her spirit has never actually been seen by succeeding Susina owners, many have heard dogs whine, their hair on end, just before the sound of her rustling skirt reached their own ears, followed by a breeze sweeping through the room.

Try as I might to evoke her presence by swinging and singing old songs I once sang as a child in my grandmother's porch swing, no spirit appeared. What I did notice was the aroma of fresh bread, so I retrieved my jacket from atop the crocheted bedspread on my four-poster bed and descended the curving staircase. In the mauve-colored living room, guests were sipping Mint Juleps or sherry as they swapped quail-hunting tales.

A large, antique table for twelve is the focus of the airy dining room, decorated in shades of blue and white and complemented by Empire serving pieces. Antique blue-and-white china graces the table. In such an intimate setting you quickly become acquainted with the guests, and before you know it, you feel as if you've been invited to a grand dinner party. I chose their Veal Cutlets served with Rice Florentine. The attractive presentation suggested a French dish, but one bite and I realized that this entrée was the embodiment of the new 'American Cuisine. That heavenly bread whose aroma had permeated my bedroom was everything I had imagined it would be. My neighboring dinner guest insisted that I taste his Stuffed Bass, which was almost too attractive to eat. I liked it so well that I knew the recipe was a must for our readers.

Pecan Pie and Apple Pie are good choices for dessert, as was my delectable Strawberry Shortcake. But the wisest choice of all is electing to experience this romantic page of our past.

Susina Plantation Inn is located on Meridian Road about 12 miles south of Thomasville and 22 miles north of Tallahassee. Follow signs off Route 319. Breakfast is served from 7:30 a.m. until 9:30 a.m., for guests only. Lunch is served from 12:00 p.m. until 2:00 p.m., reservations required. The one seating for dinner is at 7:00 p.m., reservations required. The phone number is (912) 377-9644.

SUSINA PLANTATION INN'S STUFFED BASS

2½ cups sliced fresh mushrooms
6 tablespoons butter or margarine
2 medium tomatoes, chopped and seeded
2 tablespoons parsley, chopped
1½ teaspoons grated onion
½ teaspoon lemon juice
salt and pepper to taste
2 pounds bass or pike

1 egg, beaten
¼ cup Parmesan cheese, freshly grated
½ cup fresh bread crumbs
butter
1 cup white wine
1 6-ounce package Rice Florentine, cooked
dash of parsley
tomato wedges

Cook mushrooms in medium skillet in 3 tablespoons butter or margarine over medium heat just until tender, about 3 to 4 minutes. Drain. In a mixing bowl, soften remaining 3 tablespoons butter. Stir in cooled, drained mushrooms, tomatoes, parsley, onions and lemon juice. Salt and pepper to taste.

Fillet fish and stuff with mushroom mixture. Secure with picks. Place fish in shallow, ovenproof dish. Brush fish with beaten egg. Combine cheese and crumbs; sprinkle over fish. Dot with butter as desired. Pour wine around fish. Bake at 400 degrees for 25 to 30 minutes or until fish flakes easily with fork. Serve fish with rice and garnish with parsley and tomato wedges. Serves 5.

SUSINA PLANTATION INN'S VEAL CUTLETS

1 egg
salt and white pepper to taste
1¼ pounds veal cutlets, pounded to ¼-inch thickness
½ cup bread crumbs
3 tablespoons butter
½ cup Gruyère cheese, shredded
1 6-ounce package Rice Florentine, cooked

Beat egg with salt and pepper. Dip veal in egg, then in bread crumbs, coating both sides. Cook veal in butter in medium skillet over medium heat until cooked through, about 2 to 3 minutes per side. Sprinkle with cheese and serve with rice. Serves 5.

SUSINA PLANTATION INN'S HOME-BAKED BREAD

1 package dry yeast
1 tablespoon sugar
1 cup warm water
2 cups all-purpose flour
½ teaspoon salt

In a mixer, combine yeast and sugar. Add water and let stand for about five minutes. Beat in flour with salt, a little at a time, until the dough is thick. Cover bowl and let stand in a warm place for 30 minutes. Shape into a loaf, put into a 1-pound loafpan and bake in a preheated 350-degree oven for 30 minutes. Yields 1 loaf.

THE NEEL HOUSE
Thomasville

NEEL HOUSE

Today we build a new home wherever we want, with little concern for health problems, but you need only turn back the pages of history to discover that this has not always been the case. The house of the prosperous cotton plantation owner, Elijah L. Neel, was in a prime location for the dreaded malaria. That was near the turn of the century, before modern medicine could successfully treat this life-taking fever. So Neel and his wife Martha took the only preventive measures they knew to protect their family. In 1907 they built a magnificent new home in the heart of Thomasville, far away from the feared mosquito carriers. On my visit to this beautiful house, almost entirely circled by live oaks and palm trees, I was reminded of the party at Twelve Oaks in *Gone With the Wind*.

The night I stood on the veranda next to the graceful Ionic columns of this flawlessly restored southern mansion, I felt the festive gaiety of a party in progress. Neel House was serving some of their celebrated appetizers, which gave me a chance for sampling. Sympatico with the tastes of the majority, my favorites were the rambunctiously spicy Barbecued Shrimp and the Stuffed Artichokes. Although I've made many good dishes with artichokes, I had never done anything quite so creative as stuffing them, and I was delighted to discover this recipe.

Restoration was the main topic of my discussion with Neel's granddaughter, Marguerite Williams. She is pleased with the refurbishment that has been done and told me that the front parlor was her favorite room as a child. Why? Because a visit to her grandparents meant listening to the tinkling tones of their nickelodeon.

I considered several of their lovely dining rooms for lunch the next day. I finally decided upon Williams' favorite room because it offered a good view of the silver-colored filigree moss draping the oaks. While enjoying the view, I sampled their Chicken Savannah, a moist, tender chicken in a tangy marinade. I highly recommend it. And their Crab Indigo is a most unusual way of preparing crab—a tart hint of vinegar and olive oil makes this exceptional.

Any sweet tooth will applaud either their Chocolate Silk Pie or Chocolate Nut Pie. In fact, I would wholeheartedly applaud this restaurant and inn with a standing ovation.

The Neel House is located at 502 South Broad Street in Thomasville. Lunch is served from 11:30 a.m. until 2:00 p.m. Tuesday through Friday, and dinner is served from 6:00 p.m. until 9:00 p.m. Tuesday through Thursday, and until 10:00 p.m. Friday and Saturday. Sunday brunch is served from 11:30 a.m. until 2:00 p.m. For reservations (suggested) call (912) 228-6500.

NEEL HOUSE'S STUFFED ARTICHOKES

8 ounces cream cheese
½ teaspoon basil
½ teaspoon garlic, minced
salt and pepper to taste
36 artichoke hearts, canned
2 eggs
2 tablespoons water
dash of milk
1½ cups fine bread crumbs
vegetable oil for deep frying

Whip cream cheese until smooth. Add basil, garlic, salt and pepper and mix until blended. Make a hollow in center of each artichoke by pushing center firmly to all sides. Fill the center with about 1 heaping teaspoon of cheese mixture. In separate bowl, place eggs, water and milk. Stir until blended. Dip each artichoke in egg wash, then roll in bread crumbs until sufficiently coated. Deep-fry artichokes 2 to 3 minutes or until golden brown. Drain on paper towels and then serve. Yields 36.

NEEL HOUSE'S BARBECUED SHRIMP

1 stick margarine	½ tablespoon black pepper
1 tablespoon Old Bay Seasoning	½ teaspoon basil
	½ teaspoon thyme
½ tablespoon minced garlic	½ pound shrimp, cleaned and deveined
¾ tablespoon oregano	

Melt margarine in a small saucepan and add Old Bay Seasoning, garlic, oregano, black pepper, basil and thyme, stirring until combined. Add shrimp and cook for approximately 5 minutes on simmering heat. Serves 4.

NAN'S
Valdosta

NAN'S

"**M**ashed potatoes should be prepared with canned milk or half-and-half," says Nan Wakefield, "and just a pinch of baking powder. And of course butter. Then they are nice and fluffy." My husband obligingly has another helping. "Now for roast beef," she shifts herself gingerly in her chair, favoring an arthritic leg, "I always put a little leftover coffee on my beef before I cook it. And lemon juice on chicken. It brings out the flavor."

The table around which we are sitting is spread with the Sunday buffet, served family-style with little ramekins of vegetables, platters of pot roast and fried chicken and a basket of homemade rolls. The pies and homemade ice cream wait in the wings. Nan's daughter, our waitress, asks if we want more tea. Her son Barry, the manager, hurries out to seat more customers. I inquire about Colonel Wakefield, retired now from the U.S. Air Force, and am informed that he is in the kitchen frying chicken.

"This is a family business," Nan adds, somewhat unnecessarily by this point. "We had seven children and, being a military family, always invited whoever looked hungry over to eat with us. I don't know how to cook a small amount of anything. Or what to do with leftovers. At my house, there never were any!" She laughs, and so do we, helping ourselves guiltily to just a tiny third helping of pot roast and beans. There won't be any leftovers at this table either, in spite of our vows just to nibble.

Opening a restaurant was a natural transition for the Wakefields. They bought Judge Franklin's old house, a large, rambling place built in 1909 by a family named Deal. Some of the rooms have been restored, and there are now four dining rooms downstairs and a gift shop upstairs.

Over coffee and dessert I think of Doc Holliday. Doc Holliday used to live in Valdosta before he moved to the Wild West and took up with that crowd at the O.K. Corral. Perhaps if he'd been able to eat at Nan's every Sunday he would have stayed in Georgia, married a local girl and settled down to raise a family. Then Wyatt Earp would have had to look for another sidekick, and thousands of children would have been deprived of a smashing good western tale. It pays never to underestimate the power of a good home-cooked meal.

Nan's is located at 202 East Gordon Street in Valdosta. It is open every day for lunch from 11:00 a.m. until 2:00 p.m. On Sunday there is a family-style buffet. For reservations (not required) call (912) 244-3849.

NAN'S WATER CHESTNUTS WRAPPED IN BACON

1 can whole water chestnuts, sliced in half

1 pound bacon, cut in half

Wrap the water chestnuts in bacon and broil them, turning once. Have skewers available for dipping the chestnuts in the sauce. Serves 6 to 10.

Sauce:
1½ cups pineapple juice
½ cup brown sugar

4 teaspoons cornstarch
1 tablespoon vinegar

Stir the first three ingredients together with a whisk and cook until thickened; then add the vinegar. Serve the sauce in a fondue pot.

NAN'S PRAYER FRUIT SAUCE

1 cup sour cream
2 tablespoons coconut flakes

2 tablespoons orange marmalade

Mix and serve over fresh fruit. Yields 1 ½ cups.

NAN'S EGGPLANT PARMESAN

3 eggplants, peeled and sliced
salt to taste
1 medium onion, sliced
1 tablespoon or more butter
1 pint spaghetti sauce
1 cup or more Parmesan cheese
1 cup or more grated sharp Cheddar cheese

As you peel and slice the eggplant, cover it lightly with salt. Add the onion, cover with water and steam until tender. Drain well and arrange in a buttered casserole. Cover with spaghetti sauce. Add a layer of Parmesan cheese, using more than a cup if necessary to cover the casserole. Top with a layer of sharp Cheddar, again using more than a cup if necessary. Bake in a preheated oven at 350 degrees for 30 minutes. Serves 8.

THE ATTIC
Waycross

THE ATTIC

The Attic reminds me of Hernando's Hideaway. I don't know why it should, because Hernando's Hideaway isn't even a real place, and the Attic is not only real, but good. Probably it's the stairs. To get to the Attic, you go to downtown Waycross and find a large, Charleston-limestone building with a sign reading "Carter House Family Buffet" emblazoned on the front and a staircase running up the side. Climb those stairs, open the door, and there you are.

Before you is a large, darkish room with a heart-of-pine floor and wainscotted and papered walls. A fire glints in the fireplace. The room is dotted with white-linen-covered tables and punctuated with enormous fan-topped windows. In one corner is a grill where men in white jackets are cooking meals for the guests. Other men in black jackets are carrying in salads and desserts. Beyond the grill is the bar, a narrow room where you can sit in quiet or boisterous elegance and sip a preprandial drink. The bartender that evening may be Bill Deese, who owns the place.

The restaurant serves a limited menu of steak and seafood, with an occasional offering of Canadian Backs or Baby-back Ribs, which they smoke themselves. But you won't be disappointed by the paucity of choices. The Attic confines itself to what it does well, a commendable trait in restaurants. For example, if you make reservations you will find when you sit down for dinner that the matches at your table have been inscribed with your name. The rolls are baked mere seconds before being placed before you. The cooks at the grill know exactly what the word *rare* means, so if you don't mean it, don't say it.

Do try, when eating there, to glance out the window occasionally. There seem to be more stars visible in Waycross than in other places, and the sight on a clear night is stunning, suggestive of what night must have been like before cities.

Eighty years ago people were dancing in that room, looking out at those same stars. In 1907 the Attic was the ballroom of Waycross's new Elk's Club. For thirty years, through World

War I, the Roaring Twenties and the crash of '29, people danced and drank there. Then in 1937 the Elks moved out. Maybelle Carter opened the Carter House Family Buffet downstairs and fed for a generation those who could pay and those who could not. The Carter House, which shares a kitchen with the Attic, is still serving lunch, matter of fact. The man who fries the chicken has been there for twenty-five years. Continuity seems important around there and, judging from the quality of the steak I had, they're onto a good thing.

The Attic is located at 514 Mary Street in Waycross. It is open for dinner from 6:00 p.m. until 10:00 p.m. Monday through Thursday and from 6:00 p.m. until 11:00 p.m. Friday and Saturday. Reservations are recommended, especially on weekends. Call (912) 285-5579.

THE ATTIC'S
ALMOND AMARETTO ICE CREAM

½ gallon vanilla ice cream
8 tablespoons amaretto liqueur

Almond Crunch Topping
(recipe follows)

Freeze parfait or wine glasses. Just before serving, spoon in ice cream, splash with amaretto and sprinkle with Almond Crunch Topping. Serves 8.

Almond Crunch Topping:
2 ounces sliced almonds
2 tablespoons butter

1 cup sugar
1 tablespoon water

Spread sliced almonds in a buttered pan. In a small, heavy saucepan, stir together the sugar with a tablespoon of water over low heat until the sugar has melted. Then pour it over the almonds and let harden. When the topping is completely cold, break it up with your fingers or a kitchen hammer and grind it in a blender into smaller bits. Store the topping in a covered jar in the refrigerator.

THE ATTIC'S
SHRIMP WITH CRABMEAT STUFFING

Crabmeat Stuffing:
1 stalk celery
1 small onion
½ bell pepper
1 stick butter
½ cup wine
¼ teaspoon garlic powder
½ teaspoon dill weed
¼ teaspoon pepper
8 ounces crabmeat
½ cup bread crumbs
1 egg

To prepare the stuffing, chop the celery, onion and bell pepper, and sauté them in butter. Add the wine, garlic powder, dill weed and pepper; then simmer for 10 minutes. Add the crabmeat and bread crumbs and let the mixture sit for 2 minutes. Then stir in an egg and let the stuffing cool.

4 pounds colossal shrimp (approximately 10 to a pound)
¾ cup flour
½ teaspoon baking powder
1 egg
¾ cup ice water (approximately)

Prepare the shrimp by shelling it and butterflying it, cutting it from the underside almost through, to form a pocket. Remove the vein, if necessary, by pulling it out from the underside rather than cutting the top of the shrimp. Stuff the shrimp with Crabmeat Stuffing and lay them on a tray in the freezer for a few minutes until they become manageable. (They may also be prepared ahead and frozen.) Just before serving, make up the batter by combining the flour, baking powder and egg, adding water until it is the consistency of pancake batter. Dip the shrimp in the batter and deep-fry it. (Leftover stuffing can be used to stuff mushrooms, which also can be battered and fried.) Serves 8 as an entrée or 18 as an appetizer.

BLUEBERRY HILL
Hoboken

BLUEBERRY HILL

Going to Blueberry Hill is a little like going to heaven: occasionally along the way you are bound to wonder if the place is worth the effort. Once you get there, however, all doubts are dispelled. You find such an unusual treat that before you leave you are already planning your second trip. In that respect, of course, it isn't anything like heaven at all.

Blueberry Hill sits in the middle of a piney wood near the Okefenokee Swamp. It's hard to believe that this same building was in service a hundred years ago as a tobacco barn in Pierce County. It was reconstructed on a new site as a mortar-and-log cabin with a cedar-shake roof, and seven years ago Rachel Lyons opened it as a seafood restaurant.

Part of its appeal lies in its perfect combination of crab shack and peat bog décor. My husband and I first visited it during a December rain, and Lyons hurried us across the porch, where guests can sit in fitter weather, and into the main room, where we were escorted to a place before the warm fire. In her long calico gown, leaning over to add wood to the stone fireplace, Lyons looked right at home.

My husband, whose taste in restaurants runs to French and centrally heated, looked churlish and began to feed the fire himself. I, the crab shack connoisseur, was more hopeful. The restaurant had all the requisites on my private list of a place that would fry mouth-watering shrimp and hushpuppies. I was right. But they also do fancier things well. My husband ate his Shrimp Iberville—Blueberry Hill's specialty of shrimp and mushrooms in a sherry sauce, topped with Cheddar cheese—and pronounced it delicious. Other entrées include Broiled Sea Bass, Oysters Bienville and Cajun Stuffed Shrimp. Dessert offerings are definitely in keeping with the name of the restaurant—Hot Blueberry Pie, Cheesecake with Blueberry Sauce and the Country Bumpkin, a hot blueberry muffin, served with ice cream and blueberry topping.

As we bumped our way back to the main road, my husband noted casually that though Blueberry Hill is a long way from home, it is a mere forty miles from the beach where we rent a house every summer. It would be a simple matter to drive over and have dinner a couple of times a week. Wouldn't it?

Blueberry Hill is located on Route 1 in Hoboken. The restaurant is open Wednesday through Saturday for dinner only, served from 5:30 p.m. to 10:00 p.m. On Wednesday seconds on shrimp are on the house. For reservations (recommended) call (912) 458- 2605.

BLUEBERRY HILL'S SHRIMP CHABLISIENNE

1 stick butter
1 cup diced green onions
4 tablespoons minced shallots
2 pounds shrimp, peeled and deveined

1 cup Chablis
3 ounces cognac
1 teaspoon salt (optional)
½ teaspoon pepper
2 ounces sliced almonds

Melt the butter in a frying pan and sauté the green onions and shallots until wilted. Add the shrimp, Chablis, cognac, salt and pepper, and simmer until the shrimp are opaque. Sprinkle with almonds and serve in individual ramekins with a stuffed potato and tossed salad. Serves 4.

BLUEBERRY HILL'S HUSHPUPPIES

1 cup self-rising cornmeal
½ cup self-rising flour
1 teaspoon baking powder
dash of salt

1 large onion, grated
1 egg
milk (about ½ cup)

Mix all dry ingredients together, then add the onion and egg. Add milk, stirring, until the batter is the consistency of honey. Drop it by tablespoonful into a deep fryer heated to 300 degrees and cook until golden brown. Serves 4.

BLUEBERRY HILL'S
SHRIMP AND EGGPLANT CASSEROLE

1 pound shrimp
1 pound crabmeat
4 slices white bread
4 eggs
6 ounces canned, evaporated milk
½ cup water
1 large eggplant
½ lemon
1 cup chopped celery
1 cup chopped spanish onions
1 stick butter
½ teaspoon cayenne pepper
½ teaspoon black pepper
½ cup chopped green onions
1 cup cracker crumbs (Captain's Wafers)

Peel and devein the shrimp, and pick the crabmeat. Set aside. In a mixing bowl place the bread, eggs, milk and water. Mix well and set aside. Peel and chop the eggplant and place it in a bowl of water into which the lemon half has been squeezed. In a large skillet, melt the butter and sauté the celery and onions until tender. Add the bread-egg mix, the drained eggplant and pepper to the skillet. Cook and stir until the eggplant is tender. Add green onions and the shrimp and crab, and cook until the shrimp turns pink. Place in a casserole, top with cracker crumbs and serve. (The dish can be made ahead. Add the crumbs just before serving and reheat briefly in a microwave.) Serves 6.

SEAGLE'S
St. Mary's

SEAGLE'S

There is something about Seagle's in the Riverview Hotel that draws people back to it. Just what that something is is hard to define. Built in 1916, it looks like a scene out of a Tennessee Williams play. If you look closely, you can find the watermarks from hurricanes, particularly 1964's Dora, but the lobby with its original Mission Oak furniture has weathered the elements well. At the register you'll see a cat near a Tiffany lamp, and if you look down to read Roy Crane's yellowed 1930s comic strip featuring the hotel, you'll see the same desk registry and Tiffany lamp presided over by one of this cat's predecessors. I couldn't believe it either.

Its location on the waterfront has made the hotel easily accessible to the shrimpers and other sea people who like to put in for good food in a nostalgic atmosphere. Back in the 1930s when cartoonist Roy Crane came here, he intended to stay a few days but somehow stayed for months. That's the way the Riverview is—you arrive expecting it to be just a stopover and discover how easy it is to lengthen your stay. Crane was so enamored with the Riverview that he freqently drew it in his cartoon strip. I particularly like his description of breakfast at the Riverview. A member of the hotel tells a newly arrived guest that they serve only a light breakfast, "Jist grits an' hominy an' all the ham an' eggs an' flapjacks you can eat."

Mrs. Brandon, who ran the hotel until a few years ago when her son Jerry was drawn back to St. Mary's, told me that breakfast has changed a little since Crane's days here. Although we were having lunch, the size of the platters coming out of the kitchen made it difficult to believe that much has changed in this homey dining room with its old-fashioned print wallpaper and green draperies. When you are this close to fresh deep-water Rock Shrimp, it is the item to order. The lightly fried shrimp were delightfully succulent. My platter also included some white shrimp, which I learned were so tasty because they were precooked beside the Gulf Stream. You'll also appreciate the homemade hushpuppies and French fries, which I wager taste much as they did in the

1930s. It's little things like these that continue to attract and keep people here.

If you can manage to squeeze in dessert (and you should try), I think you will enjoy their homemade Rum Cream Pie. A smoother pie you won't find. But perhaps you'd prefer to cleanse your palate with their Rainbow Sherbet.

Seagle's in the Riverview Hotel is located at 105 Osborne Street in St. Mary's. Breakfast is served from 7:00 a.m. until 11:00 a.m. daily; lunch is from 11:00 a.m. until 2:00 p.m. Monday through Friday; dinner is from 5:30 p.m. until 10:00 p.m. Monday through Saturday and until 9:00 p.m. on Sunday. Reservations are discouraged, but the telephone number is (912) 882-4187.

SEAGLE'S CASHEW SHRIMP

1 cup chicken broth, canned or homemade
¼ pound clam strips
1 tablespoon cornstarch
white pepper to taste
2 eggs
1 tablespoon water
1 cup all-purpose flour
oil for deep frying
1 pound rock or white shrimp, shelled and cleaned
½ pound rice, cooked
4 scallions, chopped
⅓ cup cashews, chopped

In a small saucepan, simmer chicken broth with clam strips, stirring frequently. Add cornstarch and white pepper and stir until smooth and slightly thickened; keep warm, stirring occasionally. In a small mixing bowl, mix eggs with water. Place flour in another small bowl. Dip shrimp in egg wash, then coat with flour and drop in hot oil until the shrimp turn golden brown. Remove shrimp and drain on paper towel. Make a bed of rice on 4 plates and spoon equal amounts of shrimp onto each. Cover shrimp with clam sauce and sprinkle with scallions and cashews. Serves 4.

SCALLOPS SEAGLE'S

2 to 3 tablespoons butter
4 scallions, chopped
½ cup fresh mushrooms, sliced
½ cup white wine
1 pound calico or fresh bay scallops
4 slices Swiss cheese

Melt butter in a skillet and sauté scallions and mushrooms until just tender. In a saucepan over simmering heat, add wine and scallops, making sure each scallop is immersed in wine. Simmer 3 to 5 minutes until scallops are white. Drain. Place scallops on plates and ladle onions and mushrooms over scallops. Lay 1 slice of Swiss cheese on each plate over top of scallops and place under broiler for 1 minute or until cheese melts. Serves 4.

SEAGLE'S RUM PIE

2 envelopes unflavored gelatin
1 cup cold water
½ cup dark rum
6 egg yolks
¾ cup sugar
1¾ cups whipping cream
1 teaspoon vanilla
2 graham cracker pie shells
grated chocolate for garnish

Soften gelatin in 1 cup cold water. Place over low heat in a small saucepan and bring almost to a boil, stirring to dissolve. Cool and add rum, stirring until well mixed, and set aside. In large bowl, beat egg yolks and sugar until very fluffy. Beat gelatin/rum mixture into egg mixture; cool in refrigerator, stirring occasionally, until almost set. In a separate bowl, whip cream with vanilla until it stands in soft peaks and fold it into gelatin mixture. Pour into pie shells and garnish with chocolate. Chill until set. Yields 2 pies.

THE KING AND PRINCE
BEACH HOTEL AND VILLAS
St. Simon's Island

THE KING AND PRINCE BEACH HOTEL AND VILLAS Sitting down for lunch, I looked through palm trees to see the ocean gently breaking upon the beach. Even on a cloudy day, that view is like having a back rub—tension just seems to ease with the flow of the tide. The view is just one reason for the feeling of tranquility at this resort.

When you first enter the hotel, the lobby's atrium features a heated pool and jacuzzi surrounded by large, lush plants, which shows you immediately that this is a hotel devoted to leisure living. Another appealing feature is the old ballroom which has been converted into a dining room. The stained-glass lunettes above the French doors provide diners with a pictorial history of the island.

My surroundings, no doubt, lent import to my luncheon choices. I thought their Neptune Burger would be a lunch-type surf and turf. Its name did not prepare me for the layers of burger, crabmeat and fresh asparagus covered with a cheese sauce and scallions. It is a powerful combination that reminds me of neither surf nor turf. Next I tried their Crabmeat Quiche, which showed me yet another expressive way to add zip to a quiche. Then I had their Shrimp Salad. Only at the beach do you get shrimp this fresh. Good chefs respect that freshness and create delicate sauces to enhance rather than mask the shrimp's natural flavor—such a sauce is served here. With my samplings, I took a bite of their honey-flavored muffins and quickly understood why guests take a few along for the road.

The next morning after an invigorating walk on the beach, I enjoyed their light breakfast in the Delegal Room, named for Lieutenant Philip Delegal, who built the first fort on St. Simons in 1736. Fearing Spanish invasion, the cunning Delegal dressed all the islanders in British uniforms, lined them single file across the beaches flanking his fort, then fired his cannons so rapidly that the Spaniards retreated from this illusion of massive troops.

Although the forts are gone, this 1935 hotel still proudly boasts Spanish colonial architecture with an elegant English colonial interior. The owners continue to update it with wonderful modern features, such as my breathtaking room on the ocean. It is no wonder that this fine hostelry has retained its former distinction as a "Kingdom by the Sea."

The King and Prince Beach Hotel and Villas is located on St. Simons Island. Breakfast is served from 7:30 a.m. until 10:30 a.m. daily. Meals are served in the Tavern from 11:30 a.m. until 9:00 p.m., and dinner is served in the Delegal Room from 6:30 p.m. until 10:00 p.m. daily. For reservations call (912) 638-3631.

THE TAVERN'S
CRABMEAT QUICHE

2 to 3 tablespoons butter
1 cup sliced red onions
1 cup julienned green and red peppers
1 celery rib, diced
½ cup chopped pimientos
4 eggs

salt and pepper to taste
12 ounces crabmeat
1 9-inch pie shell, baked
¾ pound Cheddar cheese, shredded
½ pound Swiss cheese, shredded

Preheat oven to 350 degrees. In a skillet, melt butter and sauté onion, peppers, celery and pimientos. Let cool. In a mixing bowl, beat eggs, seasoned with salt and pepper, and add to cooled vegetables. Pick crabmeat free of shells and add to the egg and vegetable mixture. Spread mixture into pie shell. Top with shredded cheeses. Bake approximately 30 to 45 minutes or until quiche is firm. Let cool slightly before cutting. If desired, heated Cheddar Cheese Sauce may be poured on top of quiche when served. Yields 1 quiche.

THE TAVERN'S KING AND PRINCE NEPTUNE BURGER

1¼ pounds lean ground beef
seasoning salt to taste
8 ounces crabmeat
12 fresh or canned asparagus spears
2 hamburger buns
1 cup Cheddar Cheese Sauce (recipe follows)
4 scallions, chopped

Divide ground beef into 4 equal portions and mold each portion into a patty and sprinkle with seasoning salt. Grill or fry hamburger on both sides until done. Set aside. Carefully pick any remaining shell bits from crabmeat and divide into 4 equal portions. Place on small plates. Steam asparagus until just tender and place 3 spears over each crabmeat portion. Grill or toast top and bottom of hamburger buns. Place cooked beef patties on top of asparagus and invert each plate onto either the top or the bottom half of a hamburger bun so that crabmeat is on top. Spoon equal amounts of Cheddar Cheese Sauce over each. Warm in a 350-degree oven, loosely covered, until hot (or in a microwave oven for 30 seconds). Garnish with scallions. Serves 4.

Cheddar Cheese Sauce:
2 tablespoons butter
2 tablespoons flour
1 cup milk
¼ cup grated Cheddar cheese

In a skillet, melt butter and stir in flour to make a roux. Slowly add milk and cheese, stirring constantly, until consistency is smooth.

THE CLOISTER
Sea Island

THE CLOISTER

When was the last time that gingersnap cookies and milk were waiting for you before going to bed? How long has it been since you had the opportunity to ride a horse along the beach at sunset? And when did you last find yourself in a breathtakingly beautiful setting, with your every need being catered to? These are but a few of the amenities that you can expect to find at Sea Island's fabulous resort, the Cloister.

Howard Coffin built his "friendly little hotel," with the help of his cousin Alfred William Jones, in 1928. It was never, even in the planning stages, considered to be just another hotel. Coffin hired famed designer Addison Mizner and insisted that the Cloister embody a lifestyle that would make it known as a "place of peace and play and freedom." As you play golf, walk beneath an avenue of majestic oaks dressed with wisps of Spanish moss, or sample the abundance of delectable food, you know that Coffin's dream is a success.

My table in the main dining room gave me an excellent view of couples dancing to the music of a live orchestra. I began with an appetizer of Tiropita, baked cheese in phyllo pastry that had a pleasant, piquant taste, which was further enlivened by a glass of 1982 Margaux. After enjoying a Lobster Bisque with Cream, I was ready for the entrée. Probably the reason I ordered a Nasi Goreng was my curiosity about the name. To my delight, this entrée of rice fried Indonesian-style with shrimp delivered a brisk tangy flavor that offset the light salad of radicchio, chicory and rocket lettuce with walnuts.

Touring the grounds, we learned that the Clubhouse has retrieved the carved ivory bust of a young slave girl sculpted by a Union soldier who spent time on the island during the Civil War. When we peeked through carved-stone, arched windows into the timeless beauty of the Spanish Lounge, which is known for its tradition of afternoon tea, we couldn't resist going in. Once inside we decided that the lounge was a tranquil place for dessert and promptly ordered a Roman Apple Cake and Rum and Spice Cake.

In spite of the wealth of activities the Cloister offers, everyone who visits raves about the food. Now I know why.

The Cloister is located on Sea Island. Breakfast is served daily from 7:30 a.m. until 9:30 a.m. in the main dining room and from 8:30 a.m. until 11:00 a.m. at the beach club; lunch is served from 12:30 p.m. until 2:00 p.m.; and dinner is served from 7:00 p.m. until 9:00 p.m. For reservations (required) call (912) 638-3611.

THE CLOISTER'S NASI GORENG

2 tablespoons diced leeks
2 tablespoons diced celery
2 tablespoons diced cabbage
1 garlic clove, chopped
2 to 3 tablespoons peanut oil
6 ounces shrimp, coarsely chopped
1 tablespoon curry powder
1 teaspoon sambal
4 cups cooked rice
1 tablespoon soy sauce
½ pound snow peas

Wash the vegetables and sauté in peanut oil in a wok or a skillet. Add shrimp, and stir until it turns pink. Add curry and sambal, stirring to incorporate. Stir in rice and add soy sauce. Taste; adjust seasonings and set aside. Steam snow peas and set aside for garnish.

Peanut Sauce:
4 tablespoons peanut butter
4 tablespoons chicken broth
1 tablespoon soy sauce

Make Peanut Sauce by putting peanut butter, chicken broth and soy sauce in a small saucepan over medium heat. Stir until smooth.

Crêpes:
½ cup milk
5 tablespoons flour
1 egg
1 egg yolk
1 tablespoon melted butter
1 tablespoon butter

Prepare crêpes by mixing milk and flour together until combined. Add the egg and egg yolk and mix in well. Add the melted butter, stirring to incorporate. Melt remaining butter in a skillet and fry crêpes very thin. Roll crêpes and slice thin. Arrange on top of shrimp mixture. Serve with Peanut Sauce and garnish with snow peas. Serves 4.

THE CLOISTER'S TIROPITA

2 ounces cottage cheese
2 ounces cream cheese
4 ounces feta cheese
2 eggs
6 sheets phyllo pastry dough (commercial)

½ cup of clarified butter
1 tablespoon butter
1 small onion, chopped

In an electric mixer combine cheeses and eggs and mix until incorporated. Take 6 sheets of phyllo and cut lengthwise into 4 strips. Brush on clarified butter. Place 1 teaspoon of cheese filling on one side of each phyllo strip and start folding like the American flag in triangles. Place on buttered sheet pan and bake at 375 degrees for 20 minutes. Melt butter in a skillet and sauté chopped onions until brown; then purée in blender and serve with tiropita. Yields 24 appetizers.

THE CLOISTER'S ROMAN APPLE CAKE

1 cup sugar
1½ cups butter
1 tablespoon salt
1 scant teaspoon mace
1 scant teaspoon cinnamon
7 eggs
2 cups skim milk
2 tablespoons soda

2½ cups cake flour
2 tablespoons baking powder
5 apples, chopped
½ cup melted butter
1 cup pecans
1 tablespoon sugar
1 tablespoon cinnamon

In an electric mixer cream sugar and butter together until smooth. Add salt, mace and cinnamon and mix well. Add eggs, one at a time. Add milk alternately with soda, flour and baking powder, and beat until well mixed. Fold in chopped apples, and pour into 3 greased and floured 8-inch baking pans. Combine melted butter with pecans and spread equally over batter. Mix sugar and cinnamon together and sprinkle over tops of cakes. Bake in a 375-degree, preheated oven for 30 to 35 minutes. Yields 3 cakes.

ELIZABETH ON 37TH
Savannah

ELIZABETH ON 37TH

If I lived in Savannah, I'm afraid I'd take its charm for granted. I'd lose that special warmth I felt when I looked through the lens of my camera and saw Spanish moss delicately framing the roof and misting across the upstairs window of Elizabeth on 37th.

Inside this elaborate mansion, copied around 1900 from a home the Gibbes family saw in Boston, you'll find an enormous fireplace in the spacious foyer. There was another, smaller, white-enameled fireplace in the fresh acanthus green dining room, where I sat within what are known as the "nooks and crannies" of older homes. When the paint was stripped from these walls, it was discovered that they were once painted red and washed with silver. That was during the time when the Sprague family, who worked with the Savannah Sugar Refinery and bought the house just before World War II, made the home a centerpiece for elegant parties.

Since black-eyed peas are almost synonymous with the South, I had to order their Black-eyed Pea Soup for my appetizer. It is a spicy soup so thick that northerners might call it a chowder. The flavor of black-eyed peas is there, but that distinct taste combines with roasted quail, fresh red pepper, wild rice and onions to form one of the heartiest soups imaginable—and perfect with a glass of Bordeaux. A great wintertime recipe!

For my entrée I chose the Oyster and Sausage Turnover, which is a terrific combination of fresh oysters and sausage tempered with three different cheeses. My Asparagus Salad accented with bacon and pine nuts and served with a light sauce was an ideal complement to the turnover.

Since host Michael Terry and the chef and owner, Elizabeth Terry, also bill the restaurant as a dessert cafe, I wasn't about to pass. I set out to try a small bit of the Savannah Cream Cake and the Light Chess Pie with Chocolate and Raspberries, but ended up eating a lot of both. The cake, featuring cream laced with sherry and a strawberry/raspberry purée, was deliciously smooth, and the pie, a tinge richer with its touch of chocolate, was superb.

Elizabeth on 37th is located at 105 East Thirty-Seventh in Savannah. Lunch is served from 11:30 a.m. until 2:30 p.m., and dinner is served from 6:00 p.m. until 10:30 p.m. Tuesday through Saturday. For reservations call (912) 236-5547.

ELIZABETH ON 37TH'S
BLACK-EYED PEA SOUP

1 16-ounce package of dried black-eyed peas
8 cups chicken broth
3 ham hocks
2 cups minced onions
1 cup minced celery
3 garlic cloves, minced
1 cup dry sherry
1 cup wild rice, cooked
½ cup fresh red peppers (or ¼ cup dried)
1 cup smoked chicken, quail or sausage, drained and diced
black pepper to taste

In a large Dutch oven, cover peas with water and let soak overnight. Drain, if necessary, the following day. Add chicken broth and ham hocks and cook, covered, for 1 hour, skimming when necessary. Add onions, celery and garlic and simmer for 30 minutes longer. Remove the ham hocks, cut meat from the bones and return meat to soup with sherry, wild rice, red pepper and smoked meat. Season lightly with black pepper. Serves 8 to 10.

ELIZABETH ON 37TH'S
OYSTER AND SAUSAGE TURNOVER

1 pound spicy, bulk sausage
1 pint fresh oysters
½ cup raw milk Cheddar cheese or mild Cheddar, grated
¼ cup cream cheese
¼ cup Assiago cheese, grated
1 pie crust recipe

Sauté sausage and drain on a paper towel. Place oysters under broiler for 1 minute to firm. Combine sausage, oysters and cheeses and drain mixture in a sieve. Prepare pie crust dough. Divide dough into quarters and roll out each quarter into a circle. Place 2 or more rounded spoonfuls of sausage mixture on half of each circle, then fold other half over mixture to form a half-moon shape, sealing edges with a fork. Continue until sausage mixture is used up. Bake at 400 degrees for 10 minutes. Serves 4.

ELIZABETH ON 37TH'S LIGHT CHESS PIE WITH CHOCOLATE AND RASPBERRIES

3 extra-large eggs
1 cup sugar
⅓ cup sour cream
¼ cup cake flour
1 pie crust, baked
1 tablespoon butter
1 teaspoon rum
¼ cup semisweet chocolate chips
½ pint fresh raspberries
½ pint heavy whipping cream
1 tablespoon Grand Marnier or crème de cassis

Separate eggs and beat whites until stiff, **but not dry.** In another bowl, beat yolks until they are a pale yellow, about 4 minutes. Add sugar and mix well, then add sour cream and cake flour until well blended. Gently fold in egg whites. Fill pie shell with mixture and bake at 325 degrees for 10 minutes until custard is set and light brown. Cool. In a small saucepan, make a glaze by melting butter and rum until blended. Remove from heat. Add chocolate. DO NOT COOK the chocolate; the hot butter/rum mixture will melt it. Stir and cool. Spread a thin layer of chocolate on the cooled pie. Cover the pie with the fresh raspberries. Whip the cream with Grand Marnier or crème de cassis and pipe or spoon over top of pie in desired design. Yields 1 pie.

THE OLDE PINK HOUSE
Savannah

THE OLDE PINK HOUSE

Offset in a square of emerald trees, the Olde Pink House glows like a rare jewel. Built in the Georgian style by James Habersham, Jr., in 1771, Savannah's oldest mansion has taken on a pink patina from the red bricks which time has allowed to seep through the white stucco. The mansion has housed many secrets, but none more important than those discussed here at the private meetings held by Habersham while trying to secure independence from Great Britain during the Revolutionary War. Even after the war, Habersham was a speaker at the state legislature and a trustee of the University of Georgia. It should be no surprise, then, that such an active man continues to make his presence known.

The chandelier was not twirling when I visited the downstairs Tavern Room for a glass of their famous Planters Punch, so I assumed that the spirit of James Habersham was content upstairs. Though the ghost has never been seen, everyone knows who lights the candles, rearranges the furniture and twirls the chandelier, because these are familiar occurrences.

Each dining room has a mellow richness that transports you back to a refined era. I favored the soft Gold Room with its handsome, eighteenth-century portraits and lovely fireplace. Dining by candlelight from hand-painted china in such a room gives you an intimate glimpse into the past. Sampling both the Black Bean and Riverfront Seafood Gumbo, I savored the distinctly herbal taste of the bean soup and was delighted with the perfect blend of cumin and vegetables in the gumbo. The little accents they provide, such as salad with a tart, creamy dressing, arriving with an ice-cold fork, create this restaurant's unforgettable personality.

Their fluffy yeast rolls are so deceptively light that you are apt to tuck more than one away. My typical Georgian supper was a delicious, rich crab cake served with asparagus, an excellent sweet ham in a delicate sauce and moist Turkey with Orange Sauce. Though the meats were exceptional, the brightest jewels were their vegetables, yellow rice tinged with turmeric and the pièce de résistance, Spiced Carrots with Hollandaise.

Ann Arnold has been creating desserts for thirty-nine years. No wonder her rich southern Sherry Trifle, crunchy Peanut Butter Pie and smooth Chocolate de Cocoa Almond Pie are edible fantasies. They, like the restaurant, are without parallel.

The Olde Pink House is located at 23 Abercorn Street in Savannah. Lunch is served from 11:30 a.m. until 3:00 p.m. Monday through Saturday; dinner from 5:30 p.m. until 10:30 p.m. daily. For reservations (preferred) call (912) 232-4286.

THE OLDE PINK HOUSE'S RIVERFRONT SEAFOOD GUMBO

1 1-pound meaty ham bone
1 chicken or turkey carcass with some meat intact
1 pound beef marrow bones
1 16-ounce can tomatoes, chopped
3 stalks celery, chopped
2 medium onions, chopped
1 large green pepper, chopped
1 teaspoon cumin or more
1 teaspoon salt
¼ teaspoon freshly ground black pepper
water to cover
1 to 2 cups beef stock
1 tablespoon butter
2½ cups sliced okra
1 17-ounce can whole-kernel corn
½ cup dry red wine
chopped parsley for garnish

Place ham bone, chicken carcass and beef marrow in a large, heavy saucepan. Add chopped tomatoes, celery, onions, green peppers and seasonings. Cover with water and bring to a boil; reduce heat, cover and simmer for 2 hours. Stir occasionally to prevent sticking. Remove the bones, leaving the meat. Add 1 cup beef stock. Stir in butter, okra, corn and wine. Simmer for 30 to 40 minutes. Taste and adjust seasonings. Garnish with parsley before serving. Serves 8.

THE OLDE PINK HOUSE'S
SPICED CARROTS WITH HOLLANDAISE

1 pound carrots
¼ teaspoon salt
½ teaspoon whole cloves
dash of cinnamon
strip of lemon peel
¼ cup brown sugar
4 tablespoons butter
1 teaspoon cornstarch, mixed with water
1 tablespoon sherry (optional)

Mustard Hollandaise Sauce (recipe follows)
chopped parsley for garnish
slivered almonds for garnish
raisins for garnish
coconut flakes for garnish

Scrape carrots and slice diagonally into 2-inch pieces. Place in a saucepan and add enough water to cover. Add salt, cloves, cinnamon and lemon peel. Bring to a boil, reduce heat and simmer for about 30 minutes, or until tender. Pour off all but ½ cup of the cooking liquid. Add brown sugar, butter, cornstarch and sherry to the pan and heat until the carrots are well glazed, stirring occasionally. Add more water or cornstarch as necessary, until glazed. Ladle Mustard Hollandaise over carrots and garnish with parsley, almonds, raisins and flaked coconut. Serves 4.

Mustard Hollandaise Sauce:
2 cups mayonnaise
¼ cup prepared mustard
¼ cup sugar
juice of 1 lemon

Mix all ingredients thoroughly in the top of a double boiler over low heat. Stir until heated through. Yields 2 ½ cups.

MRS. WILKES' BOARDING HOUSE
Savannah

MRS. WILKES' BOARDING HOUSE

People don't help one another as they once did because we are all so afraid of becoming involved. If that had been Mrs. Wilkes' decision some forty-odd years ago, I wouldn't have been fortunate enough to sit down to what a guest describes as one of her "belly-busting good" meals. When an elderly friend who owned a boarding house on Jones Street became ill and asked Sema Wilkes to help out, it seemed to Wilkes the natural thing to do, since she had always enjoyed cooking for family and friends. So, Mrs. Wilkes did get involved, an involvement that has brought her down-home cooking to the attention of *David Brinkley's Journal*, the *Today* show and myself, who heard about the restaurant up in the Georgia mountains.

Although there was no sign out front to mark the entrance to this 1870 red brick, three-story "paired house," with its double curving stairs, I could tell this was the place by the long line waiting on the sidewalk. The restaurant is on the ground floor of the house and still looks very much like an old, respectable boarding house. At first, Mrs. Wilkes fed only the boarders, but as news of her cooking spread, she grudgingly allowed a few friends and neighbors to stop by for dinner. Though no longer a boarding house, neighbors and friends continue to come, and tourists are made to feel so much at home that they leave as friends.

I sat beside Mrs. Wilkes at a large, oak table decorated with her home-grown roses and partook of the parade of bowls that made round after round. Naturally, I helped myself to a piece of her authentic Fried Chicken and refrained from another piece only because I wanted a taste of each bowl: Creole Eggplant, Pickled Beets, Green Beans, Sweet Potatoes Soufflé, Black-eyed Peas, Gravy, English Peas and Noodles, Collard Greens, Mashed Potatoes, Squash Casserole, Curried Cabbage, Cornbread Dressing and, of course, lots of hot Biscuits and Iced Tea. After a taste of Boston Cream, Coconut Cream and Sweet Potato pies, I could understand why this woman hasn't received a complaint in over two million meals, for each dish vies with the next for exceptional good flavor.

The week after my visit, Mrs. Wilkes and her daughter, Margie Martin, were scheduled to cook at Kasteel Belvedere in Brussels as America's representative of southern cooking. She told me there was no sign out front because it would detract from the home-like atmosphere. It's just this kind of attitude that can take you from a boarding house to a castle, when you're willing to get involved.

Mrs. Wilkes' Boarding House is located at 107 West Jones Street in Savannah. Breakfast is served from 8:00 a.m. until 9:00 a.m., and lunch from 11:30 a.m. until 3:00 p.m., Monday through Friday. Reservations are not accepted, but the telephone number is (912) 232-5997.

MRS. WILKES' BOARDING HOUSE'S CREOLE EGGPLANT

4 tablespoons bacon drippings
3 medium eggplants, peeled and cubed
1 teaspoon salt
½ cup diced green bell peppers
½ cup chopped onions
1 20-ounce can tomatoes
½ cup catsup
1 cup corn flakes
¼ cup or more Parmesan cheese

In large Dutch oven, heat 2 tablespoons bacon drippings and sauté eggplant with salt for about 5 minutes. In separate skillet, heat 2 tablespoons bacon drippings and sauté peppers and onions. Add to eggplant. Add tomatoes, catsup and corn flakes to eggplant and cook until flavors blend. Pour into a greased baking dish and sprinkle with Parmesan cheese. Bake in a 350-degree oven for 30 minutes. Serves 8.

MRS. WILKES' BOARDING HOUSE'S SKILLET SQUASH AU GRATIN

¼ cup butter or margarine
4 cups summer squash, thinly sliced
1 medium onion, sliced
1 teaspoon salt
dash of pepper
¼ cup water
½ cup Cheddar cheese, grated

Melt butter or margarine in a saucepan. Add squash, onion, salt, pepper and water. Cover and cook for 10 to 15 minutes, until tender. Sprinkle with cheese and serve. Serves 6 to 8.

MRS. WILKES' BOARDING HOUSE'S
ENGLISH PEAS AND NOODLES

1 10-ounce package frozen English peas
1 tablespoon bacon drippings
1 small onion, minced
1 ham hock
¼ cup mushrooms, chopped
¼ cup noodles, cooked
½ cup Cream Sauce (recipe below)

In medium saucepan, cook English peas with bacon drippings until almost tender. Add onions, ham hock, mushrooms and noodles. When ingredients are warm, add Cream Sauce and simmer until flavors are heated through. Serves 6.

Cream Sauce:
4 tablespoons butter
4 tablespoons all-purpose flour
½ pint cream or milk
4 tablespoons sherry (optional)
salt to taste
pepper to taste

In a saucepan, melt butter and add flour to make a roux. Then add cream or milk and stir until smooth and thickened. Stir in sherry. Salt and pepper to taste.

MRS. WILKES' BOARDING HOUSE'S
CURRIED CABBAGE

2 tablespoons butter or bacon drippings
6 cups shredded cabbage
1 teaspoon curry
1 tablespoon salt
salt and pepper to taste
1 cup tomatoes, chopped (optional)

In a large skillet, melt butter and add cabbage, curry and salt. Stir and cover. Cook over medium heat for about 5 minutes. Add salt and pepper to taste and, if desired, add tomatoes just before cabbage is done. Serves 4 to 5.

THE PIRATES' HOUSE
Savannah

THE PIRATES' HOUSE The lopsided door and window in the "Herb House" are mementos of the earthquake that shook this 1734 building, which now, connected to the Pirates' House, is Georgia's oldest structure. It was once the home of the gardener who worked the Trustees' Garden, the first public agricultural experimental garden in America, and it now adds the oldest footnote to the colorful inn where pirates lodged and drank.

In the Captain's Room and the Treasure Room are framed pages from Robert Louis Stevenson's *Treasure Island*. Some of the events supposedly took place here. Also in the Captain's Room, you will notice the stairway leading into the old rum cellar, where the life-sized figure of Jolly George lies sprawled at the bottom of the steps with a dagger in his back. Reportedly, shorthanded captains drugged visiting sailors, robbed them and carried the unconscious souls down through a one-block tunnel to waiting ships in the Savannah harbor. Often, unwary sailors, and supposedly even a local policeman, awoke at sea and found themselves unable to return to Savannah for months and sometimes years.

Dining in the Captain's Room, with its hand-hewn ceiling beams joined with wooden pegs, I pondered those alleged good ol' days as I foraged my way through a buffet of delectable treasures. The standouts were their Crab and Shrimp au Gratin and a unique Savannah Red Rice with just a lingering hint of herbs. Real crab lovers will appreciate the subtly seasoned Deviled Crab. And don't even think of passing this buffet table without a piece of their moist and sweet Pecan-Honey Glazed Fried Chicken. Sometimes it's difficult to find good vegetable dishes, but not here. Their Sweet Potato Soufflé with its creamy, spicy taste is another must. To balance your taste buds after that treat, help yourself to a generous portion of their Cranberry-Pecan-Orange Salad served with an Orange Juice Creamed Dressing.

Before thinking of dessert, I wanted to see their Rain Forest. This one-of-a-kind lounge is a dramatic yet soothing place to have a drink. A color cycle engineers clouds to slowly darken the room, while thunder rumbles in the background. Then, cascades of rain shower the forest only to slacken with the gradual brightening of the clouds. A really effective mood changer!

Having dessert in another of their twenty-three dining rooms, I sampled their most southern confections. Never having joined Chocoholics Anonymous, I enjoyed liberal mouthfuls of their Black Bottom Pie, enhanced with rum to bring out that rich chocolate taste. If you've a yen for creamy desserts, try Pirates' House Trifle. Also, their slightly tart Key Lime Pie really hits the mark after a seafood feast!

The Pirates' House is located at 20 East Broad Street in Savannah. Lunch is served from 11:30 a.m. until 2:30 p.m. Monday through Saturday, and dinner is served from 5:30 p.m. until 9:45 p.m. daily except Saturday, when the dining room remains open until 10:45 p.m. Sunday Buffet is served from 11:00 a.m. until 2:30 p.m. (Closed on Christmas Day.) For reservations call (912) 233-5757.

THE PIRATES' HOUSE'S
SWEET POTATO SOUFFLE

1 1-pound, 13-ounce can sweet potatoes
⅔ cup sugar
¼ cup margarine or butter
1 egg
½ cup orange juice
½ cup pineapple juice
1 teaspoon vanilla

1 8-ounce can crushed pineapple, drained (reserve juice)
1 apple, chopped fine
¼ cup pecans, chopped
1 cup or more miniature marshmallows

Preheat oven to 350 degrees. Beat sweet potatoes with electric mixer until smooth. Beat in sugar, margarine or butter, egg, orange juice, pineapple juices and vanilla, blending well after each addition. Stir in pineapple, apple and pecans. Pour into a buttered 1-quart casserole; top with marshmallows. Bake until marshmallows are brown, about 25 to 30 minutes. Serves 6 to 8.

THE PIRATES' HOUSE'S
PECAN-HONEY GLAZED FRIED CHICKEN

3½ pounds frying chicken, cut up
1 quart buttermilk
vegetable shortening for frying
½ cup butter
1 cup all-purpose flour
salt and pepper to taste
Pecan-Honey Glaze (recipe below)

Wash chicken and drain. Soak chicken in buttermilk for 1 hour. Over medium heat, melt enough shortening and butter to rise to middle of chicken in a cast-iron skillet. Put flour and seasonings in paper bag and shake 2 pieces of chicken at a time. Remove chicken with tongs and place in smoking skillet. When skillet is full, cover, lower heat and cook about 10 minutes on both sides until golden brown. Drain on paper towels. Ladle Pecan-Honey Glaze over chicken. Serves 4 to 6.

Pecan-Honey Glaze:
1 cup butter
½ cup honey
½ cup pecans, coarsely chopped

In a small saucepan, melt butter over low heat. Whisk in honey until well blended. Bring to a simmer and add pecans. Simmer 15 to 20 minutes, stirring occasionally.

THE PIRATES' HOUSE'S
KEY LIME PIE

3 egg yolks
1 15-ounce can sweetened condensed milk
rind of 1 lime, grated
½ cup fresh lime juice
1 9-inch graham cracker crust
1 cup heavy cream
2 tablespoons sugar

Preheat oven to 375 degrees. Whisk together egg yolks, milk, rind and juice until smooth. Pour into pie crust. Bake for 7 to 8 minutes. Cool on wire rack for 15 minutes, then refrigerate for 2 hours. Whip cream with sugar until soft peaks form and spread on top of pie. Yields 1 pie.

CHARLES' RESTAURANT
Lyons

CHARLES' RESTAURANT

Charles' Restaurant occupies the ground floor of the Robert Toombs Inn, which has been a hotel off and on for ninety years. When Moses Coleman built it out of wood, he unfortunately didn't take the nearby railroad into account. Cinders from the railroad caught the inn afire after only two years, and it burned to the ground. Undeterred, Coleman built again, this time of brick. In 1919 he sold the place to his niece, who ran it for a while as a boarding house. Then it became a family-style restaurant, next a clothing store. Lately it has been resurrected as a small hotel and restaurant that more than justify Coleman's perseverance. The renovation was extensive and expensively done, and the inn and restaurant have now entered the "little getaway" class of establishment, offering good food and all the amenities, plus charm.

And it *is* charming. Sitting before the fire in the little lobby-bar, sipping a glass of Chablis on a sofa Ethan Allen would be proud to claim, one could almost imagine old General Toombs, that unreconstructed radical, turning in his grave. He'll never haunt the place, though; Toombs, a former United States senator and Confederate commander, escaped to England after the "War of Northern Aggression" because he refused to pledge allegiance to the United States. If he were alive and could visit the inn named in his honor, he undoubtedly would spend a more comfortable evening than was his wont as expatriate on the lam.

The restaurant seats forty or fifty people in a room beside the lobby. There are plans to add a Victorian sun porch for additional dining space in the next year or two. You won't see much of Charles, because he'll be in the kitchen cooking your Chicken Marinara or Shrimp Scampi, or seeing that your Crabmeat Salad or Roast Beef Sandwich is properly arranged. On my last visit, I ordered the Fruit and Cheese Platter, and it was really delicious. Everything was fresh and sweet, and there was a huge platter of it, so I offered it around the table, and we all raved over the dressing. I thought about that salad for weeks, and finally called to ask Charles how he kept it so fresh. "Shoot," he said, "we cut all the fruit and cheese up after you order it. It's a job, too, I tell you. But we tried cutting it up ahead, and it just wasn't fresh enough." Then I asked him about the dressing, and he laughed. "I can't believe you're going to put a recipe that simple in a book!" he said, still laughing. But I did. All I ask is that you don't share it with just anyone. In fact, let's just keep it among ourselves, shall we? After all, do your friends or family really need to know that something so good is so easy?

Charles' Restaurant is located at 101 South State Street (at the intersection of US 1 and 280) in Lyons. Lunch is served Tuesday through Saturday from 11:30 a.m. until 2:00 p.m. Dinner is served Tuesday through Saturday from 6:00 p.m. to 10:00 p.m. For reservations (recommended) call (912) 526-4489.

CHARLES' RESTAURANT'S BASIC CRAB MIX

2 cups chicken stock
1 cup dry bread crumbs
1 bell pepper, chopped
2 onions, chopped
5 or 6 celery ribs, chopped
2 cups chopped fresh mushrooms
1 tablespoon minced garlic
⅓ cup olive oil
½ teaspoon freshly ground black pepper
½ teaspoon thyme
¼ teaspoon cayenne pepper
2 pounds crabmeat, picked
⅔ cup chopped parsley

Stir some of the stock into the bread crumbs and set them aside to soften. In a skillet sauté the bell pepper, onions, celery, mushrooms and garlic in olive oil until tender. Stir in seasonings, crabmeat, parsley, bread crumbs and stock. Adjust seasonings and liquid if necessary and simmer, stirring often, for 20 minutes. This mixture is great for stuffing flounder, mushrooms, hors d'oeuvres or crab tarts. Yields 4 to 5 cups.

CHARLES' RESTAURANT'S VEAL PICCATA

2 pounds veal scallops
1 cup all-purpose flour
salt and freshly ground pepper to taste
⅓ cup butter
juice of 1 large lemon
2 tablespoons dry white wine
⅓ cup chopped fresh parsley
2 cloves garlic, diced
3 tablespoons capers

Pound veal until very thin; dredge it in flour and season with salt and pepper. Melt the butter in a heavy skillet, adding the veal when the butter foams. Cook over high heat for about one minute on each side, until golden on the outside and still pink on the inside. Remove to a warm plate. Add lemon juice, wine, parsley, garlic and capers to the butter in the skillet and stir over reduced heat for about one minute. Taste the sauce and adjust the seasonings to your liking; then spoon sauce over veal. Serve immediately. Serves 4 to 6.

CHARLES' RESTAURANT'S FRUIT SALAD

3 cups assorted fruit, in season (melons, apples, pears, strawberries and grapes)
½ pound Cheddar, mozzarella and Swiss cheese, cut into strips

To prepare the fruit, simply cut it up and arrange it on a platter, interspersing it with the different cheeses. Serves 2.

Dressing:
1 cup sour cream   3 tablespoons brown sugar

Prepare the dressing by mixing sour cream with brown sugar. Stir and stir until the sugar has dissolved. Serve in a bowl beside the fruit.

YE OLDE COFFEE SHOP
Louisville

YE OLDE COFFEE SHOP The philosophy of Ye Olde Coffee Shop as expressed by its owner is simple: The man on the street wants good food—plain, Georgia country cooking. He doesn't want a can of beans dumped out on a plate or a fast-food hamburger, but cooking like grandma used to do. He wants fresh fish and vegetables, homemade desserts and perhaps on Friday night a nice, juicy slice of prime rib. Not coincidentally, that's just the kind of food they serve at the coffee shop.

Ye Olde Coffee Shop is housed in the Old Jefferson Hotel, a stucco structure built in the late 1920s to accommodate travelers back when much of Georgia and Florida trade went up and down Highway 1. The coffee shop starts in a corner of the hotel, where it offers breakfast to all comers in a no-nonsense but cheerful atmosphere of white cotton curtains and red-and-white checkered tablecloths. From there the restaurant meanders into the hotel proper, which it shares with a local bank. In what used to be the hotel lobby, a hundred people routinely eat a hearty buffet lunch. Beyond the former lobby lies a warren of offices and rooms in which the bankers work. It is an agreeable arrangement, since the restaurant regularly feeds the bankers, their clients and members of local civic clubs. One can borrow money over a plate of ribs, or discuss business under the original tin ceiling.

I was enchanted when I was there, sipping coffee at ten in the morning, to see people wandering around eating sausage sandwiches which they had made from a loaf of bread and a plate of leftover breakfast sausages. They would drop a dollar near the cash register and casually help themselves. The man sitting across from me was savoring one while he told me some of the history of Louisville, and only my excellent upbringing and the fact that he was bigger than I am prevented me from snatching the sandwich out of his hand and devouring it myself.

Ye Olde Coffee Shop is located at 203 Broad Street in Louisville. Breakfast is served every day from 6:30 a.m. until

10:00 a.m. The buffet lunch is served from 11:30 a.m. until 2:00 p.m. There is a special buffet every Sunday. The restaurant also is open on Friday nights from 6:00 to 9:00 serving fresh seafood and prime rib roast buffet. For reservations call (912) 625-3216.

YE OLDE COFFEE SHOP'S FRESH STRAWBERRY PIE

1 to 1½ pints fresh strawberries
1 baked 9-inch pie crust
¾ cup sugar
¾ cup water
1½ tablespoons cornstarch
2 tablespoons strawberry jello mix

Wash and drain the strawberries. Cap them and slice the large ones, leaving the small ones whole. Fill the cooled pie shell with enough berries to fill the crust, but don't mound them up. Bring the sugar, water and cornstarch to a boil and cook until thickened and clear. Remove mixture from the stove and add in the strawberry jello crystals; stir until dissolved. Pour the hot mixture over the strawberries and refrigerate at least 4 hours before serving. Top each slice with whipped topping if desired. Yields 1 pie.

YE OLDE COFFEE SHOP'S PINEAPPLE DELIGHT

2 14-ounce cans chunk pineapple
6 tablespoons flour
1 cup sugar
2 cups grated sharp Cheddar cheese
Ritz crackers
1 stick margarine

Drain the pineapple. Stir together the flour and sugar, then stir in the pineapple chunks and grated cheese. Put mixture into a casserole and crumble Ritz crackers over the top. Melt the margarine and drizzle it over the crumbs. Bake at 375 degrees for 25 to 30 minutes. This hot fruit makes a perfect accompaniment to baked ham or other baked meat. Serves 8.

YE OLDE COFFEE SHOP'S CHICKEN SALAD

1 large fryer chicken
1 5- to 6-pound stewing hen
salt and pepper to taste
1 quart mayonnaise or salad dressing

3 eggs, boiled and chopped
1½ cups chopped sweet pickles
5 celery ribs, chopped fine

Bring the fryer and hen to a boil in a large stew pot. Add salt and pepper and cook at a very slow boil until tender. The hen will take longer than the fryer, so remove the fryer when it is very tender and let the hen continue cooking until done, about 2 hours. Debone the two chickens and cut the meat into small pieces with kitchen shears. Do not use a processor. Mix the chicken with the other ingredients. Adjust the seasonings and refrigerate. Serves 8.

GOLDSMITH'S PULLMAN HALL
Augusta

GOLDSMITH'S PULLMAN HALL

Pullman Hall? Was an old train car used in the design of this Augusta restaurant? No, it's just part of proprietor Kevin Goldsmith's subtle vision. The restaurant is located downtown in a building that was erected in 1931 as a clothing store and that has passed through several different business incarnations in the intervening years. When Goldsmith first saw the old, red brick building, it reminded him of a long, narrow Pullman car—hence the name. He immediately felt that it was ripe to house a new endeavor. He reconstructed the interior with an eclecticism that juxtaposes traditional and contemporary styles. The natural brick walls provide a warm backdrop for the original, diagonal-weave hardwood floors and Tiffany-style lamps. An artistic arrangement of flags hanging from the ceiling and a collection of contemporary prints, as well as groupings of potted and hanging plants, lend an upbeat, sophisticated emphasis to the décor.

Our dinner began with three exciting appetizers: Andouille, a mild sausage; Duck Su, roast duck with a delicate gamey taste and a trace of sage; and a fabulous Boudin Blanc with Buerre Blanc, which is a hot and spicy little sausage that will wake any dormant taste bud. When I asked Goldsmith to describe his cuisine, he replied, "Food is kind of like movies here. It's served first in New York, and then it gets down to this part of the country a year and a half later."

Goldsmith, a wine connoisseur, insisted that we try a Pouligney Montrachet, which evoked a fuller flavor in the Smoked Fettucini Nova Scotia and seemed to add even more body to their hearty Shrimp Bisque.

While sampling their lamb marinated in olive oil, garlic and spices, we tried a wonderful red Chassagne Montrachet. Either the lamb or the wine could easily stand alone, but the combination was dynamite. Then, with the Tuna Teriyaki—the best tuna I've ever put in my mouth—we sipped a few drops of a California chardonnay called Russian River Ranches Sonoma-Cutrer-1, appropriately sharp to complement the sensational fresh tuna.

Goldsmith's desserts, just like their breads, are all made from scratch. And no matter what you decide to order, remember to allow room for the offerings from their dessert cart. Being someone who has never said no to chocolate, I was really torn between the Sacher Torte and Chocolate Grand Marnier Cheesecake. Both were rich and, accompanied by French coffee, they were a perfect way to end an evening in an "uptown" atmosphere.

Goldsmith's Pullman Hall is located at 724 Broad Street in Augusta. Lunch is served from 11:30 a.m. until 2:30 p.m. Monday through Friday; dinner is served from 6:00 p.m. until 10:00 p.m. Monday through Thursday, and until 11:00 p.m. on Friday, Saturday and Sunday. For reservations (suggested) call (404) 722-2805.

GOLDSMITH'S PULLMAN HALL'S
CHOCOLATE GRAND MARNIER CHEESECAKE

3 pounds cream cheese
4 cups sugar
9 eggs
grated rind of 1 orange
½ cup Grand Marnier liqueur
½ cup ground pecans
8 ounces semisweet chocolate
½ cup espresso coffee

In an electric mixer, cream together cream cheese and sugar as eggs are alternately stirred in, one at a time. Stir in orange peel and liqueur. Butter sides and bottom of a 9½- or 10-inch springform pan and coat with pecans (using more if needed). Fill pan with mixture, reserving about ⅓ cup. Melt chocolate slowly over double boiler and stir in coffee. Add chocolate mixture to remaining ⅓ cup cheesecake mixture. Pour this mixture into springform pan and swirl with a knife to make a marbled pattern. Bake in a preheated 350-degree oven for about 1 hour and 40 minutes or until done. Cool and refrigerate. Yields 1 cheesecake.

GOLDSMITH'S PULLMAN HALL'S
BOUDIN BLANC WITH BEURRE BLANC

1 pound fresh white fish, filleted	sausage casings (available at some delicatessens)
½ cup cooked white rice	2 tablespoons or more butter
salt to taste	
dash of cayenne pepper	Beurre Blanc Sauce (recipe follows)
dash of nutmeg	
dashes of available fresh herbs (basil, chives, etc.)	

Grind fish with rice in meat grinder until fine. Season with salt, cayenne, nutmeg and fresh herbs. Mix together and spoon into sausage casings and seal casings closed. Coat casings with butter and poach in a saucepan with water in a 375-degree oven until firm (45 minutes to 1 hour). Remove and grill until well marked. Ladle Beurre Blanc Sauce over sausage casings. Serves 3 to 4.

Beurre Blanc Sauce:

1 cup white wine	salt to taste
¼ cup tarragon vinegar	fresh herbs to taste (basil, chives, etc.)
1 shallot, minced	
4 sticks unsalted butter	

In a medium saucepan over medium-high heat, reduce wine, vinegar and shallots until almost dry. Lower heat and whip in cold butter, a bit at a time, stirring constantly. Remove from heat when last piece of butter is nearly melted. Add salt and minced fresh herbs to taste. Yields 2 cups.

THE KNOX TERRACE DINING ROOM
Thomson

THE KNOX TERRACE DINING ROOM

In 1865 Charles Knox was coming back from the war. On the way, he met and fell in love with a young woman. Thus inspired, he hurried home to Thomson, bought an old school and turned it into the Knox Hotel. Then he married his ladylove. Business and family prospered, and in due course the Knox children took over the business. By 1932 the grandson, Edward Knox McMannon, was ready for a change. So he and his wife, affectionately called Mrs. Mac, and his mother bought another hotel. They named it the Terrace because it had a beautiful terraced garden. For thirty years they fed and housed there the many and varied visitors to Thomson. Then, moving with the times, they built a motel and bought the Palmer home next door to serve as the dining room. Mrs. Mac is still in residence there, but her daughter Nora Poole now acts as both manager and chef, and she is stamping her own brand on the family cuisine.

The old Palmer house is one of five built in Thomson by a Mr. Bartlett, who Mrs. Mac says, "came from the North and was stranded here between the wars." Don't miss the front hall, formerly the back hall, and its "good-morning" staircase, so named because maids once used it to take late risers their first cup of coffee. The dining room is paneled and painted a dark, glossy green, and the tables, all different, are set with fine china and crystal, the result of a decision Mrs. Mac made in the 1930s: "Commercial china had changed so drastically by then, with no quality in it at all."

The food, like the dining room, is a delicious combination of traditional and new. The buffet menu varies weekly, typically featuring soup, two salads, two or three meats, five vegetables, homemade bread and dessert, usually a torte or the wonderful Lemon Bisque.

"We never thought of using anything except fresh fruits and vegetables, and of course Smithfield Ham, which is not the country kind, but a meat suitable for dining," says Mrs. Mac. Poole, who always makes the wonderful Pâté Maison herself, shares her mother's enthusiasm for fresh ingredients.

You can pay a lot more and eat not half so well elsewhere, which is probably why the citizens of Thomson and environs have been beating a path to this family's door for more than a hundred and twenty years now. When a place is well into its second century, somebody's doing something right.

The Knox Terrace Dining Room is located at 204 Jackson Street in Thomson. It is open to the public from noon to 3:00 p.m. only on Sunday. Hours vary with the season. The Knox Terrace regularly hosts private parties, hunt-club breakfasts and other special events. For reservations or to book a private dinner, call (404) 595-1529.

THE KNOX TERRACE DINING ROOM'S CHOW-CHOW

20 to 30 pounds white, hard-head cabbage
5 pounds onions
2 cups salt
2 quarts water
3 quarts apple cider vinegar
7 pounds sugar
2 pounds red peppers (or use a pint jar of sliced pimientos)
1 3-ounce box mustard seed
1 1¼-ounce box dry mustard
½ small box celery seed pickling spice tied in cheesecloth (about the size of a silver dollar)
3 pounds green peppers, diced
3 teaspoons tumeric

In a food chopper, grind the cabbage and onions and add 2 cups of salt. Soak overnight on the counter. The next morning, squeeze the cabbage and onions out in a colander. Do not rinse. In a large pot, heat the water and vinegar. Add the sugar and all the spices except tumeric. (Mix the powdered mustard in with a little of the sugar before adding it to the vinegar, so it won't lump.) Add the cabbage and onions. Cook 40 minutes and add the diced peppers, cooking 10 or 15 minutes more. Add tumeric and cook 10 more minutes. Fill sterile jars with the solids, adding enough liquid to cover the cabbage. Seal with lids. (You don't need to refrigerate jars.) Yields 12 to 16 quarts.

THE KNOX TERRACE DINING ROOM'S PATE MAISON

1 pound chicken livers
1½ sticks butter
1 to 2 garlic cloves
½ apple (cored, peeled and seeded)
1 small onion (or 2 shallots)
⅛ teaspoon basil
¼ to ½ teaspoon thyme
¼ teaspoon oregano
4 tablespoons brandy
salt and pepper to taste

Sauté the chicken livers quickly in one stick of the butter, until they are brown on the outside but still pink in the middle. Partly cover the pan, remove from heat, and cool until the butter starts to set.

In a food processor or blender, process the garlic until fine. Add the apple and onion and process. Add herbs, chicken livers and remaining butter, processing in short bursts until the mixture is creamy smooth. Add the brandy and salt and pepper to taste; process. Pour into a well-buttered mold and refrigerate overnight. Serves 8.

THE KNOX TERRACE DINING ROOM'S WALDORF SALAD

1 large cabbage
1 cup diced celery
2 cups white raisins
1 to 2 teaspoons sugar
3 red apples, partly peeled
1½ teaspoons lemon juice
1 cup mayonnaise
curry powder to taste
white seedless grapes, for garnish

Dice the cabbage. Add diced celery and raisins and sprinkle with sugar. Dice the apples and sprinkle with lemon juice. Just before serving, combine with the mayonnaise and add curry to taste. Garnish with white seedless grapes. Serve in a glass compote with lettuce or in a large, scooped-out cabbage on a crystal tray. Serves 6.

ANOTHER THYME
Washington

ANOTHER THYME

"Cheese soup?" groaned my children. "You expect us to eat cheese soup?"

"No," I said. "I expect you to wash your hair with it. Of course I expect you to eat it! Now pick up your spoons and get at it."

After the first few bites—and the choruses of "Gee, mom, this is really good!"—I felt like we were auditioning for a television commercial. I'm certain the woman who runs Another Thyme in Washington doesn't have to put up with such back talk in her establishment. She serves discriminating diners who already know that her Cheddar Cheese Soup is wonderful, not to mention her sandwiches made with homemade bread. The hot Stuffed Croissants are wonderful, and you can choose from a variety of fillings—baked ham and Swiss cheese with honey-mustard sauce, roast beef and Swiss cheese with brandy sauce and crabmeat and mild Cheddar with herb-mayonnaise sauce, to name a few of the possibilities.

Another Thyme is a long, thin restaurant on the ground floor of the old Fitzpatrick Hotel. It looks somewhat like an upended cigar box with Victorian ambiance. Pub tables and bentwood chairs line the walls, and there is a serving counter down one side. The restaurant and the antique shop next door are the finished refurbishments of an ongoing labor of love involving the whole hotel. Rod Eaton, who is doing most of the laboring, showed me around the hotel proper, upstairs. The ground floor was, as it is now, reserved for retail sales. I was amazed to see that after years of abandonment, everything is still in place—the huge pressed-tin ceiling in the old dining room, room after room of lovely wainscotting and cornices, and acres of windows with the original glass intact. When queried about the remarkable state of preservation, Eaton answered simply, "There is no looting in Washington."

Washington is in Wilkes County, one of the original eight Georgia counties. Sherman did not visit there on his famous Georgia tour, but in 1895 natural disaster conducted a little march of its own through the town square and burned half of it down. The Fitzpatrick brothers, native sons grown wealthy as merchants in neighboring South Carolina, rushed home to the rescue and built the ornate Fitzpatrick Hotel. By 1900 the Fitzpatricks were in residence, hosting drummers—the traveling salesmen of the period—and notables from Harvard who came to view the eclipse. The Harvard men had brought camping gear, expecting that the South would not be provided with hotels. When they saw the Fitzpatrick, they lost no time storing the tents and moving in. After the elder Fitzpatrick's death, the hotel was sold and renamed first the Columbus Inn and later the Washington Hotel. It closed in 1952. In its next incarnation it again will be the Fitzpatrick; Another Thyme represents the first step in that rebirth.

Another Thyme is located at 18 West Public Square in Washington. It is open for lunch from 10:00 a.m. until 2:00 p.m. Monday through Friday. Reservations are required only for large groups. Call (404) 678-1672.

ANOTHER THYME'S
CHEDDAR CHEESE SOUP

¼ cup diced celery
¼ cup chopped onions
1 cup diced carrots
1 stick butter
½ cup flour
3 cups chicken broth

2 cups milk
1 pound medium Cheddar cheese
1 pinch baking soda
salt and pepper to taste

Sauté the celery, onions and carrots in butter until soft. Add the flour and whisk until blended. Gradually add the chicken broth, whisking until smooth and thickened. Add the milk and simmer, stirring often, until thickened. Grate and add the Cheddar cheese. Mix in a pinch of soda, and add salt and pepper to taste. Simmer until cheese melts, but do not boil. Serve hot. Serves 4.

ANOTHER THYME'S CHEESECAKE

Crust:
⅓ cup light brown sugar
⅓ cup butter
1 cup flour
½ cup chopped pecans

In a food processor or blender, blend the sugar and butter until smooth. Add the flour and pecans and blend for 2 minutes more, scraping the sides of the processor. Press crust into the bottom of an 8-inch springform pan. Bake at 350 degrees for 10 minutes.

Filling:
12 ounces cream cheese
½ cup sugar
3 tablespoons milk
2 tablespoons lemon juice
1 egg
1 teaspoon vanilla

Blend all the ingredients in a food processor or blender until smooth, scraping the sides of the processor. Pour into the baked crust and bake 20 to 25 minutes in a 350-degree oven until center is firm.

Sour Cream Topping:
1 cup sour cream
1 teaspoon vanilla
¼ cup sugar

Blend all the ingredients with a spoon, and spread the topping on the cheesecake while it's still warm. (Let the cake cool for only about 5 minutes after it comes out of the oven before putting on the topping.) Yields 1 cheesecake.

INDEX

APPETIZERS
Artichoke Hearts Savannah, Atkins Park Restaurant 67
Barbecued Shrimp, Neel House 140
Boudin Blanc with Beurre Blanc, Goldsmith's Pullman Hall 192
Cajun Spicy Shrimp, Southern Trace 16
Oysters Rockefeller, Woodbridge Inn 23
Pâté Maison, Knox Terrace Dining Room 196
Stuffed Artichokes, Neel House 139
Tiropita, Cloister 164
Water Chestnuts Wrapped in Bacon, Nan's 143

BEVERAGES
Pink Carlottas, Maximillian's 43

BREAD
Cornbread, Old Mill Restaurant 31
Cornmeal Pastry, Something Special 91
Home-Baked Bread, Susina Plantation Inn 136
Hushpuppies, Blueberry Hill 151
Orange Juice Gems, Something Special 92
Sour Cream Cornbread, Farmhouse 112
Sweet Georgia Bread, Tate House 27
Sweet Georgia Brown Bread, Veranda 87
Sweet Rolls, Herren's 60

DESSERTS
Cakes:
Carrot Cake, Taylor's Trolley 12
Cheesecake, Another Thyme 200
Chocolate Chip Cheesecake, Taylor's Trolley 11
Chocolate Grand Marnier Cheesecake, Goldsmith's Pullman Hall 191
Coconut Cake, Farmhouse 111
Roman Apple Cake, Cloister 164

Miscellaneous:
Almond Amaretto Ice Cream, Attic 147
Amaretto Ice Cream Torte, Public House 40
Banana Fluff, Rankin Quarter 107
Chocolate Pâté, Mansion 52
Crème Caramel, Oak Tree Restaurant 100
Gingerbread with Whiskey Sauce, Lickskillet Farm 36
Lace Cookies, In Clover 95
Lemon Squares, Beall's 127
Pineapple Delight, Ye Olde Coffee Shop 187
Praline Tulips, Abbey 71

Pies:
Apple Raisin Pie, Stovall House 3
Chocolate Pecan Pie, Rudolph's 20
Fresh Strawberry Pie, Ye Olde Coffee Shop 187
Key Lime Pie, Pirates' House 180
Light Chess Pie with Chocolate and Raspberries, Elizabeth on 37th 168

Peach Pan Pie, New Perry
  Hotel 132
Rum Pie, Seagle's 156

Crusts and Frostings:
Banana Fluff Crust, Rankin
  Quarter 107
Coconut Frosting,
  Farmhouse 111
Cream Cheese Frosting, Taylor's
  Trolley 12
Graham Cracker Crust, Taylor's
  Trolley 11

ENTREES
Fowl:
Breast of Chicken with Eggplant
  Stuffing, Le Papillon 63
Chicken Breasts in Wine, Lick-
  skillet Farm 35
Chicken Livers, Lickskillet
  Farm 35
Chicken Fettucini, Depot at
  Covington 83
Chicken Mediterranean, Atkins
  Park Restaurant 67
Chicken Pontalba, Harry
  Bissett's 75
Chicken Duxelle, Oak Tree
  Restaurant 99
Chicken Sweet & Hot,
  Beall's 128
Fried Chicken, Hotel
  Upson 120
Hawaiian Chicken, Taylor's
  Trolley 11
Pecan-Honey Glazed Fried
  Chicken, Pirates' House 180
Marinated Chicken Livers, Pub-
  lic House 39
Roast Duckling with Orange-
  Brandy Sauce, In Clover 96
Roast Duck with "Shadows of
  the Teche" Sauce,
  Rudolph's 19
Stuffed Chicken, Stovall
  House 3

Meats:
Cuban Pork Sauté, Southern
  Trace 15
Ham and Cheddar Phyllo,
  Stovall House 4
Saddle of Beef Fiorentine, Tate
  House 27
Sweet and Pungent Pork, Fox
  Hollow 80
Veal Cutlets, Susina Plantation
  Inn 136
Veal Naturel, Bludau's
  Goétchius House 103
Veal Piccata, Charles'
  Restaurant 184

Seafood:
Cashew Shrimp, Seagle's 155
Grouper with Yellow Pepper
  Purée, Planters Restaurant 47
Nasi Goreng, Cloister 163
Oyster and Sausage Turnover,
  Elizabeth on 37th 167
Red Snapper Française,
  Bludau's Goétchius
  House 104
Scallops, Seagle's 156
Seafood à la Newberg, Wood-
  bridge Inn 24
Seafood Broccoli Casserole, Vic-
  torian Tea Room 115
Seafood Thermidor Andrews,
  Hotel Upson 119
Shrimp and Eggplant Cas-
  serole, Blueberry Hill 152
Shrimp Chablisienne, Blue-
  berry Hill 151
Shrimp de Jonghe, Herren's 59
Shrimp with Crabmeat Stuffing,
  Attic 148
Sole Oscar, Depot at
  Covington 83

Stuffed Bass, Susina Plantation Inn 135
Stuffed Flounder, Maximillian's 43

SALADS AND QUICHES
Black Pasta with Goat Cheese, Anthony's Plantation Restaurant 56
Cajun Salad, Fox Hollow 79
Chicken Salad, Ye Olde Coffee Shop 188
Crabmeat Quiche, The King and Prince 159
Fruit Salad, Charles' Restaurant 184
Lobster Chowder, Anthony's Plantation Restaurant 55
Marinated Chicken Livers, Public House 39
Mandarin Orange Salad, Left Banque 124
Oriental Chicken Salad, Mansion 51
Sausage-Cheddar Quiche, Something Special 91
Waldorf Salad, Knox Terrace Dining Room 196

SANDWICHES
Ham Delite, Rankin Quarter 107
Neptune Burger, The King and Prince 160

SAUCES, DRESSINGS AND STUFFINGS
Basic Crab Mix, Charles' Restaurant 183
Béarnaise Sauce, Harry Bissett's 76
Beurre Blanc, Goldsmith's Pullman Hall 192
Cajun Salad Dressing, Fox Hollow 79
Cheddar Cheese Sauce, The King and Prince 160
Crabmeat Stuffing, Attic 148
Crabmeat Stuffing, Maximillian's 43
Cream Sauce, Mrs. Wilkes' Boarding House 176
Eggplant Stuffing, Le Papillon 63
Garlic Butter, Bludau's Goétchius House 103
Hollandaise Sauce, Woodbridge Inn 24
Mandarin Orange Salad Dressing, Left Banque 124
Mustard Hollandaise Sauce, Olde Pink House 172
Miso Dressing, Mansion 51
Prayer Fruit Sauce, Nan's 143
Soy Sauce Dressing, Left Banque 123
Tarragon Sauce, Le Papillon 64
Turkey Dressing, Beall's 128

SOUPS AND CHOWDERS
Apricot Soup, Abbey 72
Black-eyed Pea Soup, Elizabeth on 37th 167
Cheddar Cheese Soup, Another Thyme 199
Cream of Broccoli Soup, Left Banque 123
Cream of Mushroom Soup, Maxillian's 44
Crab and Corn Bisque, In Clover 95
French Brie Soup, Abbey 71
Gin and Tomato Soup, Planters Restaurant 48
Lobster Chowder, Anthony's Plantation Restaurant 55
Maque Choux, Harry Bissett's 75
Riverfront Seafood Gumbo, Olde Pink House 171

VEGETABLES AND FRUITS

Artichoke Hearts Savannah, Atkins Park Restaurant 67
Baked Apples, LaPrade's 7
Broccoli Casserole, New Perry Hotel 132
Cabbage in Cheese Sauce, LaPrade's 7
Carrots and Rutabagas Baked with Shallots, Fox Hollow 80
Carrots au Grand Marnier, Maximillian's 44
Chow-Chow, Knox Terrace Dining Room 195
Corn Pudding, Old Mill Restaurant 31
Creole Eggplant, Mrs. Wilkes' Boarding House 175
Curried Cabbage, Mrs. Wilkes' Boarding House 176
Eggplant Parmesan, Nan's 144
English Pea and Noodles, Mrs. Wilkes' Boarding House 176
Grammy's Baked Beans, Rankin Quarter 108
Maque Choux, Harry Bissett's 75
Potato Patties, LaPrade's 8
Shredded Yams, New Perry Hotel 131
Skillet Squash au Gratin, Mrs. Wilkes Boarding House 175
Spiced Carrots with Hollandaise, Olde Pink House 172
Spinach Soufflé, Hotel Upson 120
Squash, Veranda 88
Squash Casserole, Old Mill Restaurant 32
Squash Casserole, Victorian Tea Room 116
Stir-fry Cabbage, Farmhouse 112
Stuffed Artichokes, Neel House 139
Sweet Potato Soufflé, Pirates' House 179